THE
WARWICKSHIRE
CAKES AND ALE TRAIL

First published in Great Britain by Pierrepoint Press 2011

A CIP record for this book is available from the British Library.

ISBN 978 0 9533196-6-4

Cover design by Clare Brayshaw

Typeset, printed and bound in Great Britain by:

York Publishing Services Ltd
64 Hallfield Road
Layerthorpe
York
YO31 7ZQ
Tel: 01904 431213

Website: www.yps-publishing.co.uk

THE
WARWICKSHIRE
CAKES AND ALE TRAIL

Bob Bibby

Published by Pierrepoint Press

Other books by Bob Bibby

Travel Writing

Grey Paes and Bacon: From the Heart of the Black Country

Dancing with Sabrina: The River Severn –
a Journey from Source to Sea

Special Offa: A Walk along Offa's Dyke

On the Wall with Hadrian

The Shropshire Cakes and Ale Trail

The Worcestershire Cakes and Ale Trail

Crime Fiction

Be a Falling Leaf

Bird on the Wing

The Liquidator

The Llareggub Experience

To John Rowe

Acknowledgement

Thanks for the use of particular images are due to:

Hilary Bliss for BARD logo; Nick Oliver for Ilmington Morris Men; Stratford Racecourse for their logo; Dr Adam Stuart Smith and www.plesiosauria.com for the Harbury macroplata; Ian Brown for Thwaites dumper truck; Steve Hamilton for the Red Horse of Tysoe.

Special thanks to Shona Walton, Adrian Berry and David Howe for special support and information.

"Dost thou think, because thou art virtuous, there shall be no more cakes and ale?"

Sir Toby Belch in *Twelfth Night*

CONTENTS

INTRODUCTION

Origins of the Trail

This is the third in my series of County Cakes and Ale Trails. Inspired by the success of *The Shropshire Cakes and Ale Trail* and *The Worcestershire Cakes and Ale Trail*, I decided to set about creating a similar long-distance walk in the neighbouring county of Warwickshire. The idea, as previously, was to build a seven-day circular walk, averaging about fifteen miles a day, linking up some of the small towns and ensuring a good pub for lunchtime ale, a good café for afternoon cakes and a choice of pubs for evening ales.

Warwickshire traditionally has been known as Shakespeare's county – even the local CAMRA branch names its newsletter *Shakesbeer* – and there are echoes of the great playwright everywhere you go. To judge by his characters' love of good food and drink, Shakespeare himself enjoyed hospitality and had a keen eye for everyday comestibles (Prince Hal longing for *"my sweet beef"*, Autylocus singing *"a quart of ale is a dish for a king"*). So it's no surprise to find that many pubs in the county boast of the quality of their food and that there are a number of small breweries, such as Slaughterhouse, Purity and the Warwickshire Beer Company, producing high-quality Real Ales that you may come across on the route.

In *The Shropshire Cakes and Ale Trail* I summoned Sir Toby Belch's anguished protest at the restrictions which Malvolio, that arch Puritan, was seeking to impose on Toby and his merry friends:

"Dost thou think, because thou art virtuous, there shall be no more cakes and ale?"

to support my argument for creating a walk that uses beer and pubs as central to its purpose. Sir Toby's cry echoes down the centuries against all those who would restrict the pleasures of life, who want us to drink only water and eat only salads, and whose idea of exercise is walking on a treadmill in a gym with a heart monitor attached to you. Warwickshire, of course, saw the first battle of the Civil War at Edgehill, which you will pass on the trail, so it is an even more appropriate setting for a walk that challenges Puritanism.

So *The Warwickshire Cakes and Ale Trail* also aims to respond to the doom and gloom so prevalent in modern life, as well as providing a real opportunity for those who enjoy walking to step it out beside the Warwickshire rivers and along its dales and at the same time to enjoy some of the Real Ales in some of Warwickshire's great pubs. So, although this walk is intended as a seven-day challenge, it should also be attempted with an open mind and a cheerful spirit.

Warwickshire, like most counties nowadays, is criss-crossed by a number of other long-distance paths, some of whose routes in places coincide with mine and each of which has its own attractions. The Avon Valley Footpath, the Heart of England Way, Monarch's Way, the Centenary Way and the Arden Way all coincide at times with my route. Many of these paths I have walked but none fulfilled all that I wanted, particularly in terms of offering good accommodation, good pubs and good cafés. That is why I have created my own route. Warwickshire is a largely flat county, so *The Warwickshire Cakes and Ale Trail* includes few climbs, apart from the Burton Dassett hills, and is generally on the level, following public rights of way or, occasionally, minor roads.

Warwickshire is not famous for its walking challenges. However, it is threaded with a large number of well-signposted footpaths that take the observant walker through ancient woodlands, past the haunts of birds and mammals, over rolling countryside, and beside the fast-flowing waters of the River Avon, the River Arrow and the River Stour. The best views on *The Warwickshire Cakes and Ale Trail* are from the tops of the Burton Dassett Hills, from Edgehill, from Idlicote Hill and from above Ilmington but there are other pleasing vistas throughout the journey.

The towns which I have used as the base points for each section of *The Warwickshire Cakes and Ale Trail* – Stratford-upon-Avon, Alcester, Henley-in-Arden, Kenilworth, Harbury, Kineton and Shipston-on-Stour – all have their own intriguing histories and secrets, as well as providing plenty of opportunities for walkers to take rest in a range of accommodation, take cake in the cafés and take ale in the characterful pubs and hotels. The route also leads walkers through or past many other places of interest – Norman churches, stately homes, archaeological sites, historical ruins, wonderful castles, Iron Age hillforts, and other more modern curiosities – as well as introducing them to some of the colourful characters who have contributed to the spirit of the county.

Although I have begun and ended my route in Stratford-upon-Avon, walkers may wish to find their own point of entry. Likewise, although the route is described in seven sections, each of which is approximately 15 miles long, walkers who do not have the opportunity to follow the route for seven consecutive days or who do not have the energy to cover these distances will find their own ways of managing. My hope is that any who follow in my footsteps will experience as much pleasure as I did in walking *The Warwickshire Cakes and Ale Trail*.

Planning the Walk

Those used to long days of walking on a regular basis should have no problems in covering *The Warwickshire Cakes and Ale Trail*. A reasonable amount of stamina and fitness should sustain such walkers on the journey (as will the cakes and ale!). Be aware, however, that there is a difference between a good Sunday walk and walking fifteen miles every day for a week. Getting good miles under your feet in preparation will pay off in terms of your enjoyment and comfort during your journey.

As regards equipment and clothing, I prefer to travel as light as possible but it is essential to have a good waterproof jacket and trousers. Boots (well worn in, of course) are necessary too, since the terrain in places can be quite demanding and ankles need support. If journeying in hot weather, you may be tempted to wear shorts but be prepared that at such times and in some places paths can become overgrown with nettles and/or brambles, so keep your overtrousers handy. A walking pole is a useful accessory for warding off such vegetation, as well as for shooing away inquisitive cows. Be aware also that some parts of the trail, especially where it coincides with a bridleway, can be very muddy. If arranging accommodation in advance, you might consider posting changes of clothing, new maps etc to and from where you are staying.

The walk can be done at any time of the year, though potential walkers need to beware of the River Avon flooding between Stratford-upon-Avon and Alcester, the River Arrow flooding between Bidford-on-Avon and Studley and the River Stour doing likewise in Shipston-on-Stour. The best period is probably late spring when you are likely to enjoy the fabulous blossom of the countryside at its brightest but it is an equally-pleasant experience from May to October.

Ordnance Survey Maps

The following Ordnance Survey 1:25000 maps are essential for following the route. Each has been referenced in the appropriate section.

Explorer 205: Stratford-upon-Avon & Evesham

Explorer 206: Edge Hill & Fenny Compton

Explorer 220: Birmingham, Walsall, Solihull & Redditch

Explorer 221: Coventry & Warwick

Explanatory Notes

The Warwickshire Cakes and Ale Trail guide to the walk itself is set out in seven sections, each with its own introduction which includes a gradient summary, a brief description of the terrain for that section and a mileage chart. Each section is then further subdivided into subsections of varying distances which have a narrative and diagrams of the route on one page with photographs and text about features encountered during the walk on the opposite page. The diagrams are NOT to scale but are intended to indicate the direction of the trail, particularly at junctions of paths and/or roads. The diagrams should be used in combination with the relevant Ordnance Survey Explorer Map. Because this is Warwickshire, I have included a variety of quotations from Shakespeare to amuse, illuminate and entertain you.

Each section concludes with photographs of the town where that day's walking finishes, together with a brief history of the place and an account of some of the celebrities whose names linger there. Finally, and this book would be pointless without it, there is a guide to some of the cafés and pubs in that town, together with an accommodation list and other essential information about facilities (Post Office, bank ATMs, Tourist Information Centre, Transport connections) in each. Naturally, other walkers may find different cafés and different pubs to the ones I have indicated. The selection is entirely my own and therefore entirely idiosyncratic. The accommodation list is not a recommended list but merely an indication of possibilities. Be aware, of course, that changes do occur and these listings will not be accurate for ever.

Countryside Code

* Be safe – plan ahead and follow any signs
* Leave gates and property as you find them
* Protect plants and animals, and take your litter home
* Keep dogs under close control
* Consider other people

ADVICE TO READERS

You are advised that, although every effort has been made to ensure the accuracy of this guidebook, changes may occur. It is sensible to check in advance on transport and accommodation but rights of way can also sometimes be amended.

KENILWORTH

HENLEY

ALCESTER

STRATFORD-UPON-AVON

HARBURY

KINETON

SHIPSTON
ON STOUR

STRATFORD-UPON-AVON – ALCESTER

OS Maps: Explorer 205

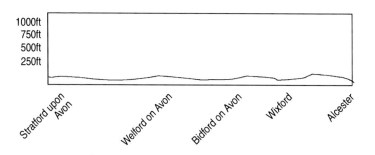

The first section of the trail is relatively easy, rarely rising above river level as it initially follows the River Avon and then the course of the River Arrow to bring you into the Roman town of Alcester.

After leaving Stratford-upon-Avon past the Royal Shakespeare Theatre and The Bard's burial place in Holy Trinity church, you pass the racecourse and then join The Greenway, created from the former Honeybourne railway line, before branching off on to the Avon Valley Way. This brings you first to Weston-on-Avon, then Welford-on-Avon with its majestic maypole and finally Bidford-on-Avon for a mid-journey break.

From there it's northwards on the Heart of England Way, calling at the attractive village that is "beggarly" Broom, going through the equally-attractive "papist" Wixford before your one slight climb of the day takes you past Oversley Castle and down into Alcester.

PLACE	DAILY MILES	TOTAL MILES
Stratford-upon-Avon	-	-
Welford-on-Avon	4.5	4.5
Bidford-on-Avon	8	8
Wixford	11.5	11.5
Alcester	14	14

STRATFORD-UPON-AVON to ALCESTER
(14 miles)

Stratford-upon-Avon to Welford-on-Avon (4.5 miles)

- Start at bottom of Bridge Street by bridge over River Avon and go along Waterside, passing in front of Royal Shakespeare Theatre, Dirty Duck and Courtyard Theatre, and at junction of roads go left on to Old Town.
- Continue on road past Holy Trinity church where Shakespeare is buried (nip in for a butcher's, if you fancy, but expect to pay). At next junction go left again into Mill Lane and, where road ends, continue forward on footpath to reach footbridge over River Avon.
- Ignore footbridge and stay on right side of river, following footpath till reaching large iron railway bridge. Ascend to right on to old railway track by Stratford-on-Avon Racecourse. Go left on railway track crossing River Avon and shortly afterwards River Stour. Continue on this track until reaching sign for Chambers Crossing Halt.

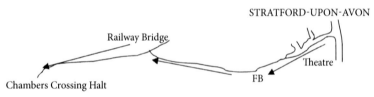

- Go right on bridleway, passing Milcote Manor Farm on right, and, ignoring tracks to right and left, reach signposted junction. Go ahead, following sign for Marcliff and shortly afterwards emerge beside All Saints church in Weston-on-Avon.
- Just past church, go right on road signposted Avon River Walk and at end of village go right, similarly signposted, on to riverside path.
- When footpath becomes surfaced track go ahead 30 yards then sharp right just past house named Riverbank. Follow clear Avon River Walk and then emerge between houses at crossroads in Welford-on-Avon, with Bell Inn to right and maypole down road to left.

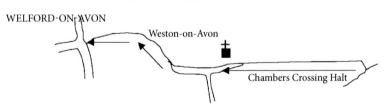

STRATFORD-ON-AVON RACECOURSE

Steeplechase racing has taken place on Shottery Meadow on the edge of Stratford-upon-Avon for over two hundred years, its first recorded meeting being as part of the Shakespeare Jubilee Festival of 1769, inspired by actor David Garrick. The two-mile Garrick Jubilee Challenge Cup, inaugurated in 1969, commemorates that event. The course has changed somewhat over the years with the acquisition of two extra fields and improvements to racegoers' facilities, including the grandstand and restaurant. This popular small course hosts nineteen meetings per year. "O! for a horse with wings!"

WESTON-ON-AVON

All Saints church is largely 15th century, though its foundation predates that time considerably. It is built of blue lias, though some of it is covered in pebbledash. On its chancel floor are memorial brasses to two Grevilles, John and Edward, both local squires and there is a medieval ashlar cross in the churchyard.

Robert Tomes (1823-1904), born in the village, became a farmer in Gloucestershire but was also a noted Natural Historian, specialising in bats, a number of new species of which he described. He wrote the sections on insectivora and chiroptera in the second edition of Thomas Bell's History of Quadrupeds. Exciting, eh?

WELFORD-ON-AVON

Welford-on-Avon is a village of attractive thatched cottages and three pubs but its three most prominent features are St Peter's church, originally 12th century, Binton Bridges, dating from the 13th century, and the site of the tallest Maypole in England, dating from the 14th century.

The Maypole is twenty metres high, its current aluminium construction replaced a wooden version that was struck by lightning.

Welford-on-Avon to Bidford-on-Avon (3.5 miles)

- Carefully cross road and go straight ahead on Church Street to reach 12th century St Peter's church. Continue on same line on to Boat Lane and at end of road go left on footpath.
- On reaching surfaced track go left 20 yards then right past caravan park to reach riverside path once again.
- Keep to riverside on well-signposted path for considerable distance, eventually passing weir and lock then crossing footbridge on to track by Birmingham Anglers Association signs. Follow track as it bends to left and up to road.
- Go right on Welford Road, passing signs that warn of flooding, towards the village of Barton.
- Go past Dovecote Caravan Park ("Dovecote Park Does Not Flood") into main village with many old stone houses (N.B. 15th century Wisson Hill and the Manor House beyond it with a plaque in its wall to 'John Payton, Anno Domini 1663').
- When reaching Cottage of Content, go right on to footpath in front of pub to return to riverside and Avon Valley Footpath.
- Follow signposted path by river then across fields to reach 15th century packhorse bridge and road. Go right over bridge into Bidford-on-Avon.

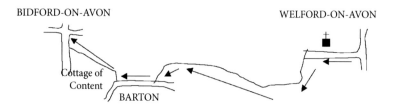

BIDFORD-ON-AVON

You enter the heart of Bidford-on-Avon on the old Roman road of Icknield Street, crossing the magnificent 15th century eight-arched packhorse bridge that takes the road over the River Avon. The bridge suggests that this was an important river crossing point for many years, the village taking its name from Byda's ford. It was destroyed in 1644 by Charles I's retreating army, rebuilt but badly damaged again in 1994 by a combine harvester.

Under the car park behind Spice Avon is the site of an Anglo-Saxon burial ground, objects from which include bronze gilded brooches, shields, pendants and rings. These beautiful pieces are on view in the Warwickshire Museum in Warwick.

On the left after crossing the bridge is The Frog (01789-772369). It is a pleasant riverside pub with its own moorings and attracts the tourist trade in summer. It serves Greene King, Hobgoblin and Warwickshire Brewery Real Ales and serves a good range of sandwiches and snacks all afternoon – highly recommended for a lunchtime break. "Eye of newt, and toe of frog."

THE OLD FALCON

In the centre of the village on Church Street is the Old Falcon, constructed in attractive Cotswold stone with mullioned windows. It was once a public house, dating back to the 13th century. It is in this latter guise that its claim to fame lies.

A group of locals from the Old Falcon calling themselves the 'Sippers' challenged a visiting group of boyos from Stratford, including the young Will Shakespeare, to a drinking contest. The Bidford team rapidly outdrank the Stratford team who were forced to sleep off the booze under a crab-apple tree in the village.

Shakespeare is alleged later to have composed this scurrilous verse about Bidford and other neighbouring villages:

Piping Pebworth, Dancing Marston,
Haunted Hillborough, Hungry Grafton,
Dodging Exhall, Papist Wixford,
Beggarly Broom and Drunken Bidford.

Bidford-on-Avon to Wixford (3.5 miles)

- Opposite The Frog take unnamed road, passing Methodist Church on left to reach B439.
- Go straight across on to signposted path and at next road junction go straight across again passing Westholme Court bungalows.
- At next road junction go left and at end of road go right on Westholme Road.
- Where road ends, go straight ahead on path to reach Jackson's Meadow. Go left then immediately right at T junction.
- Just past Broom Nursery, follow road rising to bridge. At top of bridge go left on descending path.
- Cross first road in Broom and take path through metal gate to next road with Broom Tavern on left.
- Go straight across on to surfaced track and at next junction go ahead again on path.
- Continue on clearly-waymarked path through fields and over stiles, passing Moor Hall JCB storage on left.
- Continue on clear path over stiles to reach metal gate, then go left and cross two footbridges to emerge on roadside with Fish Inn at Wixford immediately opposite.

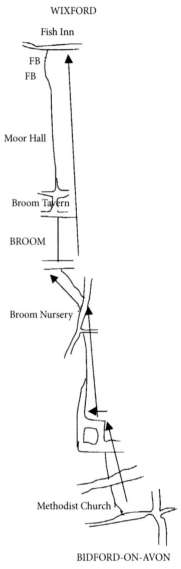

WIXFORD

Fish Inn

FB

FB

Moor Hall

Broom Tavern

BROOM

Broom Nursery

Methodist Church

BIDFORD-ON-AVON

BROOM

The "Beggarly Broom" of the rhyme is a complete misnomer, as you will see from the many attractive old buildings in this village. These include the stone-built house that was once St Matthew's church, several black and white houses and others with thatched roofs. The oldest building is the 16th century redbrick and half-timbered Broom Tavern, formerly a farmhouse, as was the Broom Hall Inn. The former sports a sign depicting Shakespeare and friends sleeping under a crab-apple tree (yes, this one will run and run).

WIXFORD

"Papist Wixford" (please keep up) owes its tag probably to its connection with the Catholic Throckmortons who were lords of the manor. Its 12th century church, St Milburga's, has two simple Norman doorways and Warwickshire's most magnificent brasses on the 1411 tomb of Thomas de Cruwe and his wife. The graveyard has an ancient yew tree and a 17th century stable where the priest kept his horse.

There are two inns in the village, the Three Horseshoes, where a blacksmith's forge once stood, and The Fish that overlooks the River Arrow. "This is no fish but an islander."

OVERSLEY CASTLE

The white-painted Oversley Castle is in the parish of "Dodging Exhall" and you have to dodge the village on your route in order to glimpse this building. It is not a castle but an embattled folly, built at the whim of the Prince Regent in the early part of the 19th century. The future George IV, enamoured of the Marchioness of Hertford who lived in nearby Ragley Hall, thought that the view from the Hall would be enhanced by the addition of a castle, and so it came to pass. Oversley Castle was revamped in the 1930s by the grocer David Greig, making it look more like an Odeon cinema. "Lord, what fools these mortals be."

Wixford to Alcester (2.5 miles)

- Go ahead through Fish Inn car park to gate and path alongside caravan park.
- Continue through two gates. After second gate go right at fork in paths.
- At crossroads in paths by St Milburga's, go straight across through blue gates past Oversley Farm.
- Keep on surfaced track twisting to reach gates of Oversley Castle and go left following waymarking sign.
- At next fork in paths go right. After passing house follow track bending left towards two large green silos.
- Pass silos and Lower Oversley Lodge farm and at T junction go right.
- Two thirds down descending track, go through metal gate on left on to footbridge over A46 into Oversley Green.
- At T junction at end of Primrose Lane go right on Mill Lane. Just after postbox go left on Stratford Road and over bridge.
- Go straight across next road to take path through park.
- At end of park go right and follow Malting Mill Lane (once homes of needlemakers), bending to reach St Nicholas's church and centre of Alcester.

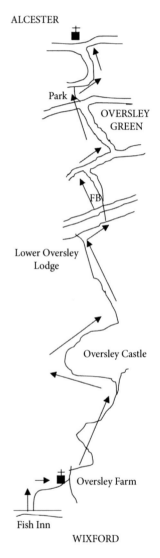

ALCESTER

Park

OVERSLEY
GREEN

FB

Lower Oversley
Lodge

Oversley Castle

Oversley Farm

Fish Inn

WIXFORD

ALCESTER PIX

Alcester Town Hall

St Nicholas

Fulke Greville Tomb

High Street Mosaic

Three Tuns

Roman Museum

ALCESTER STORY

"All on a nice modest scale. Nothing imposes itself. Nothing hurts"
Nikolaus Pevsner

Although there is evidence of the area being inhabited in pre-historic times, Alcester's origins really lie in Roman times. Some time in the first century AD Roman soldiers were building Icknield Street and the place where it crossed the old Saltway from Droitwich at the junction of the rivers Alne and Arrow became the site for the settlement known as Alauna, modern-day Alcester. There has been much recent archaeological excavation in Alcester and the recently-opened Roman Alcester exhibition in the centre of the town gives an excellent guide to these finds.

It was the Anglo-Saxons who gave the town its name of Alcester, recognising its Roman origins. A Benedictine monastery was founded there in the 12th century by Ralph de Boteler and in the 13th century it received a Royal Charter to hold a weekly market and an annual fair. In 1299 the town was given the right to appoint its own Court Leet to deal with minor crimes and the Court Leet still meets, though mostly it is for ceremonial purposes, such as Ale Tasting. St Nicholas's church, originally 11th century, was substantially rebuilt in the 18th century and has an unusually-sited clock facing askew down High Street.

The linen industry was central to Alcester's wealth from the 13th to the 15th century, later joined by knitting and glove-making, but the town was also an important staging post from Roman times for the transportation of salt from Droitwich, from the 17th century for the needlemaking industry of the Arrow Valley and later for the growing merchant class, because of its situation on the main route between London and Holyhead. After the Dissolution of the Monasteries, Henry VIII made the first Sir Fulke Greville lord of the manor. The tomb of him and his wife lies in St Nicholas's church in the town.

Modern-day Alcester is a busy market town in the heart of Warwickshire, its High Street exhibiting much history through its attractive old buildings. Its proximity to the West Midlands conurbation makes it an attractive commuter town, though it has developed a range of smaller industries and commercial businesses on its trading estates, as well as encouraging tourism. It is also the headquarters of Great Britain and Ireland Rotary International.

ALCESTER CELEBRITIES

Nicholas Throckmorton (1515-1571)
Sir Nicholas Throckmorton of Coughton Court just north of Alcester played a key role in the relationship between Elizabeth I and Mary Queen of Scots. He was involved in various court intrigues, which led him to be thrown into the Tower of London. On Elizabeth's accession, he was Ambassador to France between 1559 and 1564, where he became acquainted with Mary, Queen of Scots. His attempts to find a rapprochement between Elizabeth and Mary failed, however, and he was imprisoned for a time in 1569 in Windsor Castle.

Fulke Greville (1554-1628)
Born to one of England's richest families, Fulke Greville was a poet of some note but is more famous for his biography of his friend, Sir Philip Sidney. The two of them were deeply involved in the life of Queen Elizabeth I's court. MP for Warwickshire and Chancellor of the Exchequer, Fulke Greville was knighted in 1597, made first Baron Brooke by James I and given Warwick Castle, which he substantially restored. He was murdered therein by one of his servants, who thought he was going to be cheated in his will.

Frederick Jackson (1860-1938)
Born at Alcester Lodge Farm, Frederick Jackson was a noted Arctic explorer. In 1893 he completed a 3,000 mile sledge-journey across the frozen tundra of Siberia and Lapland, publishing an account of his journey entitled *The Great Frozen Land*. Three years later he was given command of a Royal Geographical Society expedition to explore Franz Josef Land in the Arctic Ocean, showing that the area was an archipelago not a continent. Jackson Island in the archipelago is named after him.

David Greig (1865-1952)
Greig's might by now be as famous a name as Sainsbury's, for both families began their chain of stores at about the same time. In fact, it is reputed that David Greig once employed John Sainsbury. At one time Greig had 250 stores in the south of England but gave much of his wealth to assist the underprivileged. During World War 2 he established an egg-packing business in Alcester and, on his wife's death in 1947, he was responsible for creating the trust which opened and maintains Greig Hall as a community centre.

ALCESTER CAKES

VENUE XPRESSO & ALCESTER ART, *High Street*
Coffee shop and original art gallery, offering sandwiches, homemade soup, homemade cakes, coffees and teas. Everything except the coffee is locally-sourced in this cheerful and warm café.

TUDOR ROSE TEAROOMS, *High Street*
Traditional food along with an extensive take-away menu. Recently-opened bakery offering a range of bread, cakes, savouries, ice cream, sandwiches and drinks.

WELCOME CAFÉ, *Priory Road*
Offers hot and cold sandwiches, baguettes and paninis, plus coffees and teas in unpretentious surroundings opposite town's library.

ALCESTER ALE

THE THREE TUNS, *High Street*
Old-fashioned bar with flagstones, low Jacobean beams and wattle-and-daub walls. No piped music, no food, no pool table – just like pubs used to be. Range of Real Ales including Hobsons, Jousters plus varying Guests, plus fruit wines. CAMRA recommended.

THE HOLLY BUSH, *Henley Street*
17th century pub with five panelled rooms, including central bar, and garden. Good range of food, ever-changing Real Ales including Banks's and Brakspear, plus farmhouse cider. Folk evenings and beer festivals. Regular winner of CAMRA local Pub of the Year.

THE TURKS HEAD, *High Street*
Reopened as a pub in 1999 after years as antique shop. Wooden floors, crackling fires and leather sofas. Range of Real Ales including Timothy Taylor, Wye Valley plus Guests. Excellent range of food. Chess and backgammon played. Regularly featured in Good Pub Guide.

THE LORD NELSON, *Priory Road*
Old beams and a real fire. Range of Real Ales, including Greene King IPA and Bombardier, good food and a warm welcome promised. Traditional pub games, including proper billiards, available.

ALCESTER ACCOMMODATION

The Old Barn, 7 Swan Street, Alcester, B49 5DP (Tel: 01789 762010)

The Lord Nelson, 69 Priory Road, Alcester, B549 5EA
(Tel: 01789 762632)

The Globe Guesthouse, 54 Birmingham Road, Alcester, B49 5EG
(Tel: 01789 763287)

The Swan Hotel, Swan Street, Alcester, B49 5DP (Tel: 01789 766999)

The Roebuck Inn, Birmingham Road, Alcester, B49 5QA
(Tel: 01789 762410)

Travelodge, Birmingham Road, Alcester, B49 6AA
(Tel: 01789 766987)

ALCESTER SERVICES

Post Office: High Street

Banks with ATM: Lloyds, HSBC, Halifax and Barclays in town centre

Tourist Information Centre: in Library (Tel: 01789 762430)

Transport connections: regular bus service to Redditch and Stratford-
on-Avon, where there are mainline railway stations.

ALCESTER – HENLEY-IN-ARDEN

OS Maps: Explorer 205 & 220

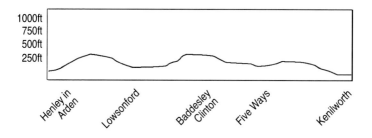

The second section of the trail follows the route of the Arden Way for much of the journey, ending up appropriately in Henley-in-Arden, once at the heart of the Forest of Arden. Leaving Alcester, the route takes you out into the country before bringing you back down one of Warwickshire's Unclassified County Roads into the village of Coughton, dominated by Coughton Court – home for generations of Catholic Throckmortons, many of whom have been involved in court intrigues over the centuries.

The trail continues its northwards direction following the River Arrow as far as Studley, a town formerly famed for its needlemaking artisans, before veering eastwards past the Studley Castle Hotel, once a Young Ladies Agricultural College, and on to the village of Ullenhall, where the Winged Spur offers a welcome mid-journey break.

Finally, it's a journey across meadows and beside streams to bring you into the town of Henley-in-Arden, famous for its still-active Court Leet and its delicious ice cream.

PLACE	DAILY MILES	TOTAL MILES
Alcester	-	14
Coughton	3.5	17.5
Studley	6	20
Ullenhall	9.5	23.5
Henley-in-Arden	14	28

ALCESTER to HENLEY-IN-ARDEN
(14 miles)

Alcester to Coughton (3.5 miles)

- Leave Alcester by taking Kinwarton Road from St Nicholas's church, passing Town Hall and later Rotary International building.
- Shortly after passing mini-roundabout at Kinwarton Farm Road, take waymarked path to left, initially through woodland then on rising track to pass trig point.
- Continue on path through two gates. After slight climb, go through gate in hedge on left then follow right field boundary.
- On reaching road, go left 30 yards then right through gate and climb across field to further gate.
- Go straight ahead, crossing wide track, then follow right field boundary. On reaching signposted gap, go through and follow left field boundary. On reaching house, go left through gate then through further gate on to road.

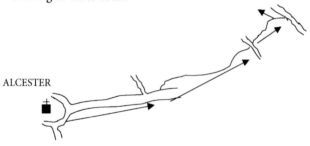

- Go left on road to New End Farm. Just after road to Shelfield Green, go left on broad track (Unclassified County Road).
- Keep on this track to eventually reach road by ford. Cross road and take footbridge on right to rejoin road into Coughton.

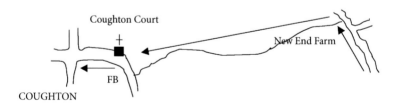

COUGHTON COURT

The fine Warwickshire stately home Coughton (pronounced "coat-un") Court dates back to the fifteenth century. The oldest part of the house is the huge and imposing Gatehouse, originally built around 1510. The stone-built house has been added to and altered over the centuries, notably after the damage inflicted on it by Cromwell's troops during the 17th century Civil War and by a local mob at the time of the 1688 Glorious Revolution.

The house contains one the finest collection of Tudor memorabilia in the country, including the chemise worn by Mary Queen of Scots when she was executed and the Throckmorton coat, made between sunrise and sunset in one 1811 day from the sheep shearing to the finished coat. This enabled the then baronet, Sir John Throckmorton, to win a thousand guinea bet.

THE THROCKMORTONS

Coughton Court has been the family residence of the Throckmorton family since 1409. They are one of England's leading Catholic families, which has inevitably led them to being at the centre of many religious disputes. Francis Throckmorton was executed in 1583 for his part in the plot to replace Elizabeth with Mary Queen of Scots. The sister of Thomas Throckmorton was married to Robert Catesby, the leader of the 1605 Gunpowder Plot. No wonder then that the place fell foul of the local populace during the Civil War and the Glorious Revolution. "As flies to wanton boys are we to the gods".

Coughton Court was gifted to the National Trust in 1946 with the Throckmorton family being given a 300-year lease. They are still there, with Clare McLaren-Throckmorton and her daughter Christina Williams responsible for the beautiful gardens. They even have a pub named after them – The Throckmorton Arms.

Coughton to Studley (2.5 miles)

- On reaching A435 in Coughton, go right along front of Coughton Court grounds. Just past entrance for cars, go right again in front of house to gate and then through two further gates.
- After second gate, go left to follow field boundary round two sides of field to further gate. Go diagonally right across field to further gate, then follow path alongside River Arrow to green metal footbridge.
- Continue on path to reach St Leonard's church at Spernall.
- Past church go left on road, then left at T junction for 30 yards. Just before road bridge, go right on broad track towards Spernall Hall Farm.
- Go past farmhouse then through wooden gate followed by three metal gates. Continue on path to further gate, then go left to cross footbridge.
- Follow right field boundary to end of hedge, then go right through gate alongside River Arrow. When river finally bends left, go straight ahead across field, aiming for cemetery beside church.
- Continue to site of old town of Studley, keeping cemetery on right, to reach gate on to road.
- Go right on broad rising track to reach Studley Castle Hotel.

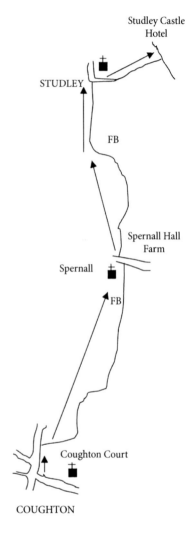

SPERNALL

The tiny village of Spernall, depopulated by the Black Death in the 1340s, contains little nowadays other than the redundant church of St Leonard. Originally Norman, the church was rebuilt in 1844 but made redundant in 1972; it is now the workshop of the artist Nicholas Jones, who works in wood, plaster and stone.

St Leonard's has had two interesting incumbents as its vicars. In 1536 Humphrey Stile was described in a Puritan tract as "a parson dumbe and unlearned a common alehouse haunter and of suspected life". His 1670s successor was Henry Teongue, whose amusing diaries of his time spent as a naval chaplain show that he had a robust appetite for life, enjoying the songs, toasting, party games and a lavish officers' dinner prepared for the birthday of Charles II. "What a piece of work is man."

STUDLEY

The modern town of Studley sits alongside and to the west of Icknield Street but the remains of the Priory and Castle and the parish church are further east, indicating that the original settlement was closer to the River Arrow. Studley was known for its expertise in making needles, both for

sewing and for surgical purposes. This expertise began with the settlement of exiled Huguenot refugees in Elizabethan times.

The Augustinian Priory was founded in the 11th century and dissolved in 1536, with the prior John Yardley receiving a pension of £15 a year. Nothing remains of the Priory today although its stone was used in many other buildings.

The original Studley Castle was Norman but it was in ruins when it was purchased and expensively remodelled by Francis Lyttleton-Holyoake in 1833. Sadly, he died broke, as did the person who bought it. In 1903 the Countess of Warwick bought it as an Agricultural College for Young Ladies, as which it remained until 1963 when it became a training college for MG Rover employees. It is now a hotel and conference centre.

Studley to Ullenhall (3.5 miles)

- Cross entrance driveway to hotel and continue on broad track past several houses to reach Castle Farm. Just before farm grounds go through black gate on right and then diagonally across field to gate in opposite corner.
- Follow track to right, bending left. At signposted fork, keep straight ahead to gate then cross field to further gate. Take rising path over Mars Hill to gate, then follow right field boundary to two further gates.
- Go diagonally right across field to two successive gates, then follow left field boundary to further gate. Follow right field boundary past pool on right, with Morton Bagot Manor beyond, and through two gates. Go diagonally right to gate and follow track to road.
- Go left into farmyard, bearing right then going diagonally left through gate. Follow same diagonal line across field, heading for houses, to reach road.
- Go left and just past Chester's Green Cottages go over stile on right and follow right field boundary to signposted gap in hedge.
- Go through and follow left field boundary rising to gate. Go through two fields with gates between then further gate to pass Cadborough Farm buildings on left and reach A4189 via stile and gate.
- Go left on road for 100 yards then right through copse to stile. Take rising path to gate on left of large house on to road. Turn right towards Ullenhall. Opposite church, go left on path leading to centre of village and Winged Spur.

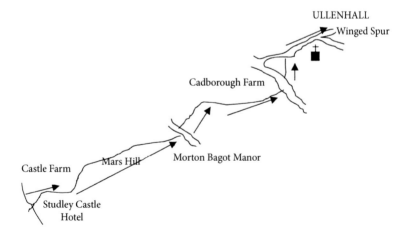

MORTON BAGOT MANOR

Morton Bagot Manor House was an 18th century farmhouse expanded in the early 20th century by a Birmingham industrialist from the motor trade, Sir Oliver (later Lord) Lucas. During the Second World War, Lucas served as chairman of the National Joint Council of the Motor Vehicle Retail and Repairing Trade, as a reward for which work he was ennobled in 1946 by Clement Atlee. He went on to serve as Lord-in-Waiting, Captain of the Yeomen of the Guard and Parliamentary Secretary to the Minister of Transport but fell out with the Labour Party over nationalisation and resigned office.

ULLENHALL

The village of Ullenhall is almost certainly of Saxon origin but only became a parish in 1861 and had its first church, St Mary's, in 1875. Worshippers before that time attended the Old Chapel, recently renovated for the Millennium, on the hillside within the village bounds. The Coffee House and Village Institute opened in 1883 to provide food and education for the poor of the village.

The fire-ravaged ruins of The Barrells contain the story of Lady Henrietta Knight, Lady Luxborough, who was forced to live there permanently by her husband because of an alleged affair with a vicar named Dalton. At The Barrells she established a literary coterie that included William Somerville, William Shenstone and Richard Jago. Do you care?

The Winged Spur (01564 792005), which takes its name from the emblem of the Knight family, is first mentioned in 1797. It opens every lunchtime from 12 to 2.30, serving a range of Real Ales including Ruddles, Everards and Greene King and a good selection of bar snacks. "I have no spur to prick the sides of my intent."

Ullenhall to Henley-in-Arden (4.5 miles)

- From front of Winged Spur go left past War Memorial and at T junction go left again for 100 yards to gate and path.
- Go diagonally right across field, rising to gate. Cross road to further gate and continue on rising path to gate by signpost for Dean's Green and Blunt's Green.
- Go straight ahead on Chapel Lane and, where road forks, go right towards chapel. Pass to left of chapel through two gates then take gradual descent through two fields with gate between to reach gate on to road.
- Go left on road and then right at first road junction. Keep on road as it bends right at Dean's Green and then passes under railway bridge. At T junction go straight across on to path over stile and continue through woodland over stiles to footbridge.
- Go diagonally right across field to stile.
- Go left over footbridge then diagonally right across long field, passing pool on right, to double stile and plank bridge. Continue ahead to stile in right corner of field on to road opposite Waterloo Cottage.
- Go right for 50 yards then right over footbridge to gate. Cross field to further gate then follow stream through two long fields with footbridge between. Midway through second field go right through gate to cross stream bed to stile. Go left beside stream through long field to gate. Keep on path to footbridge up to A3400.
- Cross road and go right, then left past Henley Palace into Camp Lane. 100 yards after last house go right over stile and follow right field boundary through three fields with gate and stile between to further stile.
- Go right over stile across field then left over stile and follow path to stile on to road. Go right and immediately left on A3400 and follow into Henley-in-Arden.

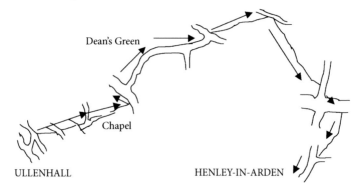

Dean's Green

Chapel

ULLENHALL

HENLEY-IN-ARDEN

HENLEY-IN-ARDEN PIX

Guildhall

White Swan

St Nicholas

Henley Ice Cream

Market Cross

Heritage Centre (Joe Hardy House)

HENLEY-IN-ARDEN STORY

"In Tudor times this was the centre of the mighty Forest of Arden – the setting adopted by Shakespeare for his play 'As You Like It'."

The earliest records of Henley-in-Arden stem from immediately after the Norman Conquest, when Thurstan de Montfort built his motte and bailey castle on the hill known as The Mount that overlooks the present town. In 1220 Henry III granted Peter de Montfort permission to hold a weekly fair and market in Henley, by which time the two adjacent manors had become one. In 1265, as a reprisal for Peter de Montfort taking arms against the king, Henley and its castle were burned down. By 1296, however, it had recovered, was awarded borough status and subsequently became an important market town, though it had no church of its own until 1367.

In the old Market Place in the town centre is the remains of a rare 15th century Market Cross. The Market Hall was the meeting place for the Court Leet, which acted as the main form of local government from the 11th to the 19th century. Curiously the Court Leet has remained in Henley, largely for ceremonial functions, although it is nowadays able to represent the town within Warwickshire. The current Court Leet meets regularly at the Guildhall and annually elects its officers, such as Ale Tasters, Brook Lookers, Butter Weigher, Town Crier etc.

Henley-in-Arden is in reality one mile-long road, High Street, all of which is a Conservation Area. It contains many buildings of architectural interest, including the 15th Century Guildhall, the 16th century coaching inn the White Swan, the 15th century church of St John the Baptist and several half-timbered buildings.

As well as its many attractive buildings, Henley-in-Arden has long been known for its famous ice-cream shop. This dates back to the 1930s when two brothers, confusingly named Fathers, purchased the Tudor Dairies in the town and began experimenting with ice cream, using a secret recipe of their mother's. The reputation of Henley Ice Cream grew until in 1937 it was voted the best ice cream in the United Kingdom. When the brothers retired in 1959, the business was bought by Ross Foods, who turned it into a business manufacturing ice cream in bulk for supermarkets. Fortunately, Henley Ice Cream is now back in private ownership, serving the needs of local people and visitors to the own. It is not to be missed.

HENLEY-IN-ARDEN CELEBRITIES

Peter de Montfort (1205-1265)
The de Montforts were the most important family in the early post-Conquest days of Henley-in-Arden, their family seat being Beaudesert Castle, earthworks of which are still evident. Peter de Montfort was an important ally of Simon de Montfort (no relation) in his attempts to gain greater power from the monarchy for the great barons. He saw important service with Henry III, escorting the future Edward 1 to Spain for his marriage to Eleanor of Castille. He died, with Earl Simon, at the Battle of Evesham in 1265.

Benjamin Beddome (1717-1795)
Benjamin Beddome was born in Henley-in-Arden and became a noted Baptist minister who served as minister at Bourton on the Water in Gloucestershire for 55 years. He is famous for the number of hymns he composed – some 800 in all, with catchy titles such as *Behold the Eunuch When Baptized*, *This World's a Dreary Wilderness* and *Let Party Names No More*.

William James (1771-1837)
William James may be justly considered to be the father of the railway system. He trained as a solicitor but became fascinated by the horse-worked railways used in mining districts in the north of England. In 1821 he visited George Stephenson and saw his steam locomotive at work, which further fired his enthusiasm and he proposed the creation of a line between Liverpool and Manchester but, because of delays, he was removed from that work. He was succeeded, much to his anger, by George Stephenson. There is a memorial to him in the town.

Joseph Alexander Hardy (1923-present)
In 1992 Joe Hardy, an American billionaire, bought the title of Lord of the Manor of Henley-in-Arden at auction, admitting that "he wanted to buy some class". He is the founder and CEO of '84 Lumber' in Pennsylvania, the American equivalent of B&Q, and of the family-run Nemacolin Woodlands Resort. He has established a trust fund to maintain the Henley Heritage House museum, now known as Joe Hardy House, while handing the title of Lord of the Manor to his daughter, Mrs Robin Hardy-Freed. At the age of 84, Joe Hardy married 22-year-old Kristi Georgi, only to divorce her 107 days later for "irreconcilable differences".

HENLEY-IN-ARDEN CAKES

THE HENLEY BAKERY, *High St*
Homemade cakes and bread made on premises. Coffee shop open from 8.30 to 4.00, serving sandwiches, baguettes, homemade cakes etc plus teas and coffees.

HENLEY ICE CREAM PARLOUR & TEAROOMS, *High Street*
Award-winning café dating back to 1930s offering 41 flavours of ice cream, plus sandwiches and paninis, and cream teas in the afternoon.

AU PETIT VILLAGE, *High Street*
Continental-style café, serving freshly-made sandwiches, handmade patisserie, luxury teas and speciality coffees from 9-5 Monday to Saturday

HENLEY-IN-ARDEN ALE

BLACK SWAN, *High Street*
Very welcoming traditional pub with good basic food at reasonable prices. More pub grub than gastropub. Serves Batemans XB, Highgate and Banks's Mild Real Ales.

BLUEBELL, *High Street*
Terraced black beam and white rendered building. Award-winning pub serving good quality food and drink in a comfortable environment but quite upmarket and can get busy. Serves Purity UBU, Weatheroak Victoria Works and Church End Fox Without A Hat Real Ales.

THREE TUNS, *High Street*
Small terraced pub, with a white rendered front and black beams at the gable. Serves London Pride, Shakespeare County and Weatheroak Icknield Pale Real Ales. No food.

WHITE SWAN, *High Street*
Oldest pub/hotel in town, dating back to 1550s. Has had many famous visitors including poet William Shenstone and lexicographer Samuel Johnson. Serves Cornish Tribute, Purity Gold, Black Sheep Bitter and Banks's mild Real Ales and good range of bar food.

HENLEY-IN-ARDEN ACCOMMODATION

Bridge House Hotel, 289 High Street, Henley-in-Arden, B95 5DH
(01564 794469)

White Swan Hotel, 100 High Street, Henley-In-Arden, B95 5BY
(01564 792623)

The Old Rectory, Preston Bagot, Henley-in-Arden, B95 5EB
(01926 843023)

Village Garden B&B, Liveridge Hill, Henley-in-Arden, B95 5QX
(01564 783553)

HENLEY-IN-ARDEN SERVICES

Post Office: High Street

Banks with ATM: Lloyds, Barclays and HSBC, all in High Street

Tourist Information Centre: Library, Guildhall, High Street
(01564 792965)

Transport connections: mainline railway station.

HENLEY-IN-ARDEN – KENILWORTH

OS Maps: Explorer 220 & 221

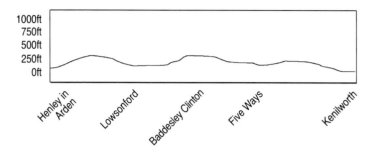

This section takes you out of Henley-in-Arden past the mound on which Beaudesert Castle stood and across country up to the viewing point beside Preston Bagot church. Then it's down to the canalside for a pleasant stroll beside the Stratford-upon-Avon Canal to Lowsonford for piemen and then on to Kingswood Junction for a merger with the Grand Union Canal. You then leave the waterside to inspect the stately home of Baddesley Clinton, another refuge for Catholics in the bad old days.

Your mid-journey break (take your own sandwiches) is at the unusual and interesting The Case is Altered in the roadside settlement that is Five Ways. Then it's across country through Haseley Green and Beausale to rejoin the Heart of England Way as it leads to the magnificent Kenilworth Castle and on into the town itself.

PLACE	DAILY MILES	TOTAL MILES
Henley-in-Arden	-	28
Lowsonford	3	31
Baddesley Clinton	6	34
Five Ways	8.5	36.5
Kenilworth	13.5	41.5

HENLEY-IN-ARDEN TO KENILWORTH
(13.5 miles)

Henley-in-Arden – Lowsonford (3 miles)

- Leave Henley-in-Arden via Beaudesert Lane beside church of St John the Baptist on High Street. Just past church of St Nicholas, ignore Arden Way sign and go straight ahead on waymarked path. Continue past school and school playing field.
- Just past playing field go right at junction of paths to cross road and reach gate into Jubilee Park. Go left on stepped path through woodland to stile at top of steps.
- Go right and immediately left over stile to follow left field boundary to road. Cross road and continue on same line over three stiles to cross track.
- Keep on same line over two stiles and at next stile go right in coppice for 30 yards then left over stile and straight ahead over two fields with stiles between.
- Go through plantation via metal gates and after second gate go ahead in direction of farm buildings and church, aiming for metal gate.
- Continue past Church Farm on left through several gates to reach road with Old Rectory opposite. Go straight ahead on rising path to church in Preston Bagot.

- Pass All Saints church on left to reach road. Go straight ahead through gate and take descending path through two fields to reach footbridge over stream.
- Go right to find towpath beside Stratford-upon-Avon canal and go left on towpath. Follow towpath, passing Yarningale Aqueduct to reach Lowsonford.

PRESTON BAGOT

Preston Bagot is a tiny village with houses scattered around its hillsides and meadows, the second part of its name coming from a certain Ingram Bagot who grabbed the land in the Norman conquest of England. The hilltop church of All Saints dates from the 12th century and boasts some windows by Burne-Jones as well as a tall pointed bellcote. It affords spectacular views of the surrounding countryside. "Let every eye negotiate for itself."

STRATFORD-UPON-AVON CANAL

The Stratford-upon-Avon Canal runs for just over twenty-five miles, taking boats from Stratford north to join the Grand Union Canal at Lapworth and then on to join the Worcester and Birmingham Canal at the outskirts of Birmingham. Built between 1793 and 1816 it contains fifty-five locks, one tunnel and three aqueducts, including the Yarningale Aqueduct on the route. There are several barrel-roofed lock-keepers' cottages along the canal, built around 1811 with bridgebuilding techniques to save money.

By the 1940s the canal had fallen into disuse but restoration began in 1961, using volunteers and prisoners from Winson Green prison and it was reopened in 1964. Its restoration was a turning point for the waterways movement in Britain.

FLEUR DE LYS, LOWSONFORD

The Fleur de Lys is the pub where Fleur de Lys pies, famous in pubs and chip shops throughout the land, had their origin. The landlord between

1950 and 1958, a certain Mr Brookes, started cooking his Steak & Kidney and Chicken & Mushroom pies at a time when pub grub was no more than a packet of crisps and a pickled egg. His creations became famous and he took over a factory to produce his infamous pies. Legend has it that pies containing unknown meats are called Fleur de Lys because the French king once had a pie baked with the body parts of an English spy and sent it to the English king. Who ate all the pies then? "He hath eaten me out of house and home."

Lowsonford to Baddesley Clinton (3 miles)

- Continue on towpath from Lowsonford, passing under M40.
- Pause at Dick's Lane Bridge and turn handle on post to hear the story of Tom the Lengthman.
- Continue to reach Kingswood Junction, where the Stratford-upon-Avon canal joins the Grand Union canal.
- Go right via water facilities on to link canal, then right again on towpath, passing under railway bridge.
- At Bridge 37 go left on to Grand Union canal towpath and follow up to Bridge 65.
- Go up to road and go right, passing Navigation Inn at Lapworth.

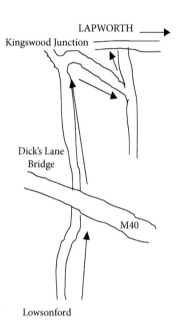

- Immediately opposite Manor House, go left on wide track, then through stables area with gates either side.
- After second gate go diagonally right across field to metal gate in opposite corner.
- Follow right field boundary to further gate then cross field to gate on drive to Baddesley Clinton manor house.

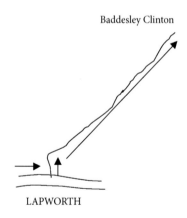

GRAND UNION CANAL

The Grand Union is, as its name suggests, a union of several separate canals that was finally completed in 1929 to create a direct route between Birmingham and London, with arms and links to Leicester and Nottinghamshire. The advent of the railways and later of improved road transport led to considerable upgrading

of the Grand Union, with the creation of double locks, the widening of bridges, the replacement of narrow gauge with broad gauge locks and the strengthening of banks with concrete. These improvements meant that boats in excess of sixty tons could travel between Birmingham and London. At the same time the Grand Union Canal Carrying Company was formed to create the largest fleet of working narrowboats in the country.

The Grand Union was a vital route during the Second World War for carrying coal to Birmingham, which was the centre of arms manufacture, and it remained active and busy commercially until the 1970s. Nowadays, however, it is largely used by pleasure craft. "The barge she sat in, like a burnish'd throne, burnt on the water."

BADDESLEY CLINTON

The moated manor house of Baddesley Clinton, dating from the 13th century but largely unchanged since 1634, was from the early 16th century until the 1940s the home of the Ferrers family. Like many Warwickshire great families, the Ferrers were staunch Catholics and the manor house became known as a hide-out for Catholic priests and Jesuits, using the priest-holes and secret passages incorporated in the building. One of these priest-holes was a toilet from which fugitives could escape down a rope to the house's former sewers.

One of those who found refuge at Baddesley Clinton was the poet and priest Robert Southwell, whose Burning Babe poem was used as a stimulus by Shakespeare in Macbeth. After Southwell's execution, his poems were shown to Elizabeth I who is said to have been moved to show "signs of grief" – an emotion rarely displayed by the Virgin Queen. "Frailty, thy name is woman."

Baddesley Clinton to Five Ways (2.5 miles)

- From gate go right up drive to Baddesley Clinton, passing car park.
- Just before entrance to Baddesley Clinton manor house, go left on signposted path to St Michael's church.
- Leave church by two gates. At second gate go straight ahead to reach road.
- Cross road on to bridleway leading into Hay Wood.
- Go straight ahead in Hay Wood on main track, ignoring paths to left or right and crossing surfaced track half-way through wood.
- Eventually arrive at signposted gate out of wood. Go diagonally right across field towards farm buildings.
- Go right past buildings then left and left again to emerge on drive of Wood Corner Farm.
- Go right on drive to reach A4141 (Birmingham Road) and go right again.
- Follow footpath on road into Wroxall and, just before Wren Hall, go right on signposted path through gate.
- Continue on broad track to fork in paths by signpost. Go left along line of oak trees to reach gate by oddly-shaped walls of Wroxall Abbey/The Mansion.
- Continue past main entrance to The Mansion and go straight ahead across long field to gate, then across further field to gate on to road.
- Go left on road to reach Case is Altered in Five Ways.

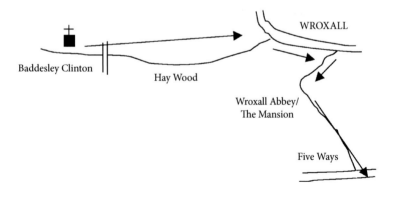

34

WROXALL ABBEY

Wroxall Abbey owes its origins to Sir Hewe de Hatton who, while imprisoned in the Holy Lands for seven years during the Crusades, had a vision of St Leonard who promptly beamed him home to "Wrocheshale". Unrecognised at first by his wife, he proved his identity with a ring and then founded the priory for Black Nuns in gratitude. A stained glass window in the mansion depicts this legend. A later prioress was Isabella Shakespeare, Will's aunt – but they all say that!

After the dissolution in 1534 the priory was almost all broken up and replaced with a redbrick manor house that was in 1713 bought by architect Sir Christopher Wren as his country home. In the 1860s the estate was bought by wealthy industrialist and banker James Dugdale, who built a new mansion in the then-fashionable Victorian Gothic style. That is the building that in the 1930s became Wroxall Abbey School for Young Ladies and is now The Mansion, a hotel and leisure centre, specialising in posh weddings and the like. "Some Cupid kills with arrows, some with traps."

THE CASE IS ALTERED

One of those little gems loved by Real Ale enthusiasts and buried way in the Warwickshire countryside, The Case is Altered owes its name to curious circumstances. The inn sign that used to hang outside portrayed two bewigged lawyers but the law was always against this pub. Known originally as The Case (possibly because it was no bigger than a small suitcase), the inn was regularly refused a licence because it was too small, until an enterprising landlord added a very small extension to the building. Result? Licence granted and pub name changed accordingly to The Case is Altered (01926-484206).

No food here, other than crisps, but also no children, no dogs, no computers, no music, no fruit machines and no mobile phones. Small bar billiards table but requires old sixpences to run it (from the bar). Excellent range of Real Ales, including Greene King, Hook Norton, Sharp's Doom Bar plus guest beers from local breweries. Not to be missed.

"Let's kill all the lawyers."

Five Ways to Kenilworth (5 miles)

- Continue past Case is Altered to reach junction of Case Lane with Five Ways Road. Go right on Five Ways Road and pass houses to reach Shaws Lane.
- Go left on Shaws Lane and at end of road cross A4141 on to signposted path.
- Go through field with two gates between, then cross track to Haseley Hall Farm to reach footbridge over stream
- Go diagonally left on rising path over field to stile. Continue on same line through next field to stile in opposite corner and footbridge.
- Continue on rising path to stile on left of houses to reach road in Haseley Green. Go straight across road through gate on to bridleway.
- Continue through series of three gates to reach next road. Go left on road to enter settlement of Beausale.
- Keep on road to take second road on left, signposted Beausale. At top of rise in road, go right on signposted path.
- Where broad track bends left, go straight ahead on rising path through two fields to further gate. Continue on same line through next two fields with gates between.
- Continue on clearly-signposted path (look for yellow-topped posts), eventually bearing slightly left with magnificent view of Kenilworth Castle ahead.
- Continue on path aiming for Kenilworth Castle, till reaching car park for castle and main entrance driveway. Go left out of driveway then right at bridge to path through Abbey Fields, passing Swimming Baths and Abbey ruins, to reach A452.

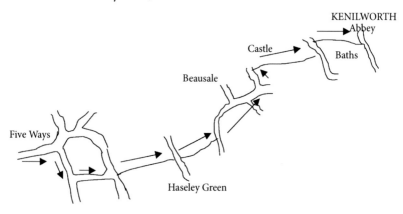

KENILWORTH PIX

Kenilworth Castle

Elizabethan Garden

Leicester's Gatehouse

Clock Tower

Famous Virgins & Castle

Abbey Ruins

KENILWORTH STORY

"...procure me license to attend the Summer Progress unto your lordship's most beautiful and all-to-be-unmatched Castle of Kenilworth."

Sir Walter Scott

The history of Kenilworth is inextricably entwined with that of its premier landmark, the glorious Kenilworth Castle, including its recently-recreated Elizabethan Garden with its bejewelled aviary and 18-foot-high Carrara marble fountain, all of which was originally built by Robert Dudley in his attempted wooing of Elizabeth I at his infamous 19-day booze-up of 1575. The castle was begun by Geoffrey de Clinton, Henry I's treasurer, in 1120 and was considerably strengthened by King John. In 1266 at Parliament Piece just off the modern Coventry Road Henry III held a parliament that was to provide a means for the barons to regain their lost lands, thus taking another step towards parliamentary democracy. The land is now open space and is being turned into a nature reserve.

The inheritance of Kenilworth Castle in 1563 by Robert Dudley, Earl of Leicester and the great favourite of Elizabeth I, saw its next great development. As well as the Elizabethan Garden, Dudley lavished huge amounts of his wealth on the building, adding the mansion-size Leicester's Building, complete with a dancing chamber for the queen's use, and a splendid new entrance, known now as Leicester's Gatehouse. Although it survived the Civil War largely untouched, the castle was made indefensible afterwards and never again featured in the history of the kingdom. It is now managed by English Heritage.

Abbey Fields in the centre of Kenilworth was once the site of an Augustinian Priory, originally created by Geoffrey de Clinton. After Henry VIII's Dissolution of the monasteries if 1538, it fell into disrepair and some of its stone was used by Robert Dudley in his revamping of Kenilworth Castle.

Another of Kenilworth's claims to fame is the set of thatched cottages in the grounds by the castle known as Little Virginia. Here, it is claimed, the very first potatoes brought from America by Sir Walter Raleigh were planted. In the 19th century with the coming of the railway the town boasted a large number of mansions, all of which have now disappeared, replaced with housing estates. The town is now largely a dormitory town for commuters to Birmingham, Leamington Spa and Coventry

KENILWORTH CELEBRITIES

Simon de Montfort (1208-1265)
Simon de Montfort is now thought of as one of the founders of modern democracy because he called for an elected parliament. He married Henry III's sister and was given Kenilworth Castle by the king but he fell out with his brother-in-law and became the leader of the group of barons seeking greater influence in England. Simon defeated Henry III at the battle of Lewes but was defeated and killed at the Battle of Evesham in 1265.

Robert Dudley (1532-1588)
Robert Dudley, Earl of Leicester, was by reputation Elizabeth I's favourite squeeze. He was widely believed to have been her lover for many years and he certainly harboured hopes that she would marry him. In 1575 he sought to woo her at his ancestral home of Kenilworth Castle with a 19-day binge-drinking party that included a Lady of the Lake, a swimming papier-mâché dolphin with a little orchestra in its belly, fireworks, masques, hunts and popular entertainments like bear baiting. She never gave in, although, after his death, she kept his last letter to her in a treasure-chest beside her bed until her own death fifteen years later. Make of that what you will.

Sir Walter Scott (1771-1832)
Walter Scott's novel *Kenilworth* derives from an old ballad that was one of Scott's favorites and tells the story of Amy Robsart, the first wife of Robert Dudley. According to Scott, Dudley felt he had to keep his marriage a secret, either to maintain his position at court or because of his long pursuit of Queen Elizabeth herself. After a series of intrigues, Amy dies in a fall at her country house. In order to write his novel, Scott stayed in the Famous Virgins and Castle Hotel.

Andrew Davies (1936-present)
Andrew Davies is a prolific writer and screenwriter, most notable for his adaptations of classic works of fiction such as *Pride and Prejudice*, *Vanity Fair*, *Sense and Sensibility*, *Middlemarch* and *Little Dorrit*. He was a lecturer at Warwick University for many years but left in 1987 to become a full-time writer. He has written children's books (*Marmalade Atkins, Conrad's War, Alfonzo Bonzo*), television series (*A Very Peculiar Practice, Game On*) and plays for television, as well as adapting other writers' work for television and cinema. He can often be seen walking his dog in Kenilworth where he lives.

KENILWORTH CAKES

ROCKING HORSE COFFEE SHOP, *Talisman Square*
Serves morning coffee, light lunches and afternoon teas, plus an all-day breakfast. All cakes are homemade and very popular.

ESCAPE COFFEE SHOP, *Abbey End*
Independent coffee shop offering Fairtrade, organic and locally-sourced produce, prepared fresh to order. Attractive ambience with modern canvas art around its walls.

TIME FOR TEA, *Castle Hill*
A quiet, family-run, traditional tea shop selling fresh, homemade soups, cakes and light lunchtime meals.

KENILWORTH ALE

CLARENDON ARMS, *Castle Hill*
Recently extensively refurbished inn that serves good food at reasonable prices and several Real Ales, including Hook Norton, Black Sheep and Timothy Taylor Landlord.

THE ROYAL OAK, *New Street*
Known for its welcoming atmosphere and for being a real local pub. Decorated with some West Bromwich memorabilia but never mind. Serves several well-kept Real Ales, including Black Sheep, Bombardier, Timothy Taylor Landlord and Ansell's Mild.

OLD BAKERY, *High Street*
Restored former bakery in heart of town. First pub in Warwickshire to go completely non-smoking. Attractive patio around an old well. Serves Hook Norton, Timothy Taylor Landlord and other Real Ales. Very popular with fans of good beer.

THE FAMOUS VIRGINS & CASTLE, *High Street*
Very large pub but divided into lots of smaller areas. Serves good pub food, including Filipino and Japanese items, and several Real Ales, including Everards Tiger, Beacon and Sunchaser. Very popular and can be busy but worth the effort.

KENILWORTH ACCOMMODATION

Aaron Quince House, 29 Moseley Road, Kenilworth, CV8 2AR
(01926 858652)

Abbey Guest House, 41 Station Road, Kenilworth, CV8 1JD
(01926 512707)

Avondale B & B, 18 Moseley Road, Kenilworth, CV8 2AQ
(01926 859072)

Cottage Inn, 36 Stoneleigh Road, Kenilworth, CV8 2GD
(01926 853900)

Enderley Guest House, 20 Queens Road, Kenilworth, CV8 1JQ (01926
855388)

Ferndale House, Priory Road, Kenilworth, CV8 1LL (01926 853214)

Hollyhurst Guest House, 47 Priory Road, Kenilworth, CV8 1L
(01926 853882)

Loweridge Guest House, Hawkesworth Drive, Off Tainters Hill,
Kenilworth, CV8 2GP (01926 859522)

The Cottage, 56 High Street, Kenilworth, CV8 1LV (0192 511617)

KENILWORTH SERVICES

Post Office: Station Road

Banks with ATM: Lloyds and HSBC in The Square, NatWest in
Warwick Road

Tourist Information Centre: The Library, Smalley Place
(01926 748900)

Transport connections: regular bus services to Coventry, Leamington
Spa, Stratford-upon-Avon and Warwick for mainline railway stations.

KENILWORTH – HARBURY

OS Map: Exploroer 221

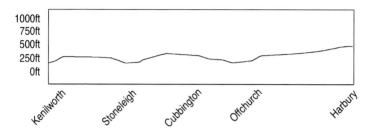

The sensible route out of Kenilworth would be through the grounds of Stoneleigh Abbey but sadly, despite huge a mounts of public money being spent on its refurbishment, there is no public way through, so you have to follow instead the somewhat circuitous route taken by the Centenary Way to pass through the village of Stoneleigh.

Over the River Avon again and then more paths and bridleways bring you to the outskirts of old Cubbington, now more a suburb of Leamington Spa but once an identifiably separate village. A late-morning stretch from there brings you into the ancient settlement of Offchurch, allegedly founded by the Mercian King Offa where The Stag offers a mid-journey and actual mid-trail break point.

A long stretch of open country, taking in the old drovers' route known as Welsh Road and another of Warwickshire's Unclassified County Roads takes you through the little settlement of Ufton with its Lady Godiva connections and then southwards into Harbury with its six pubs – what choice!

PLACE	DAILY MILES	TOTAL MILES
Kenilworth	-	41.5
Stoneleigh	3	44.5
Cubbington	6	47.5
Offchurch	8.5	50
Harbury	13.5	55

KENILWORTH to HARBURY
(13.5 miles)

Kenilworth to Stoneleigh (3 miles)

- From car park by church on A452 go left and then right at traffic lights on to New Street, until reaching fork in roads just after Royal Oak pub. Go right on to Manor Road. At postbox go left on Tainters Hill then immediately right on Lower Ladyes Hills.
- Where road ends, continue straight ahead through Kenilworth Common Nature Reserve (look out for lots of butterflies). Keep going under railway bridge, with stream on right, to reach gate on to Common Road.
- Go right and at next road junction go right again on Dalehouse Lane. After 80 yards go left on Knowle Hill. Climb to reach Frythe Close, then take waymarked footpath left, winding through woodland, to emerge on Kenilworth Golf Course.
- Follow signs through centre of golf course (keeping eyes and ears open) to eventually reach gate to exit course. Go through gate then left to end of hedge. Go straight ahead over two fields, crossing driveway between, to reach gate on to surfaced track. Continue ahead past Kingswood Farm, following footpath signs to metal gate.
- Follow left field boundary to further gate beside A46. Go left along right field boundary through two fields with gate between to reach stile. Take stepped path up to road. Go right on road and cross over A46.
- Continue to next crossroads, then go right on road signposted Stoneleigh Abbey. After 50 yards, go left through gate and follow right field boundary through two gates. At second gate, go left on footpath across field to further gate. Follow clear path weaving between houses to emerge by Holly House in Stoneleigh.

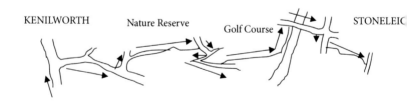

JANE AUSTEN AND STONELEIGH ABBEY

Stoneleigh Abbey was the family home of the Leighs, who were relatives of Jane Austen. Jane with her mother and sister arrived here in 1806 in the company of the Rev. Thomas Leigh, her mother's cousin, in order to take charge of his inheritance of the estate. While she was staying here, Jane became intrigued by the house, the parkland and the estate in general and she used them subsequently in her novels.

Jane Austen tours, led by locals dressed up as if for a BBC costume drama, are on offer every Wednesday and Sunday at 1.00 pm.

After the dissolution of the monasteries the estate was purchased by Sir Thomas Leigh, then Lord Mayor of London who had a house built there. Stoneleigh Abbey is now owned by a Trust, which is why you can't see it or even walk through its grounds without paying for the privilege, despite £10 million of public money used to refurbish it. Protest!

STONELEIGH PARK

Stoneleigh Park ("the home of rural excellence") is an 800-acre events centre owned by the Royal Agricultural Society of England. It hosts events throughout the year, including such as the Shorthaired and Ragdoll Cat Show, the Spring Alpaca Festival, the Jaguar International Spares Day and, of course, the Royal Show.

The village of Stoneleigh has no pubs. There used to be three but they were closed down by the then Lord Leigh when some local drunks laughed at his daughter cycling to church on a tricycle. Honestly, it makes you weep. "Sweet are the uses of adversity."

Stoneleigh to Cubbington (3 miles)

- Cross road and continue straight ahead, passing St Mary's church on left, to take footbridge over River Sowe. Keep on path rising over Motslow Hill. At top of hill go left at signpost to gate into woodland and further gate to road.
- Go right on road for 100 yards to waymarked path to Stareton on left through two gates. Go straight over middle of field, descending gradually to two footbridges.
- After second footbridge over River Avon, continue ahead climbing through two gates on to road in Stareton. Leave Centenary Way signs and go right past Park Farm House for 100 yards.
- Opposite cottages take broad track (Unclassified County Road) and continue to reach A445, Leicester Lane.
- Go left 30 yards to path on right just beyond cottage and follow over stiles and through gates to reach Coventry Road by farm.
- Go straight across over plank bridge to gate. Follow right field boundary to footbridge. Go along hedge and woodland to signpost. Go right 100 yards then left to eventually reach gap in hedge and go down to road.
- Go straight across and continue on path as it becomes a road in Cubbington to emerge beside King's Head and St Mary's church.

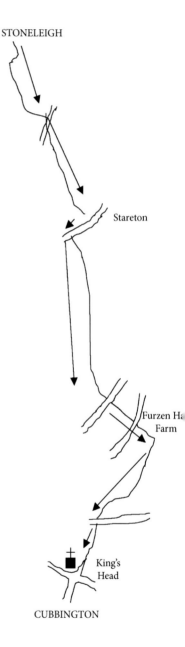

STONELEIGH

Stareton

Furzen Ha Farm

King's Head

CUBBINGTON

CUBBINGTON

The large village of Cubbington is now little more than a suburb of Leamington Spa but it can trace its origins back to the 1086 Domesday Book. The red sandstone church of St Mary is Norman in origin and Jane Austen's brother James was vicar here from 1792 to 1820. On the wall of the chancel is an unusual memorial to Captain Abraham Murcott, who was lost at sea off the Scilly Isles in a dreadful storm in 1702.

Because of a fight involving two local men some years ago, the men of the village have become known as Cubbington Earbiters. A better reputation was won during the Second World War when the villagers opened their already overcrowded houses to evacuees from Coventry, Birmingham and London.

Cubbington is the home of Thwaites Dumpers, makers of dumper trucks 'beyond imitation', created in 1938 and now exporting dumpers and small excavators all over the world. Thwaites Dumpers employ over two hundred staff.

The Warwickshire Beer Company, producers of a range of Real Ales including Shakespeare's County, Lady Godiva, King Maker and Falstaff (couldn't resist them, could they?) is also based in Cubbington.

JOSEPH RUSSELL OF CUBBINGTON

Joseph Russell (1760-1846) was a remarkable farmer and inventor who was honoured by the Society of Arts and Sciences for his revolutionary ideas about enhancing agricultural practice. He farmed in Cubbington, where he introduced Leicestershire sheep into Warwickshire and conducted some cross-breeding experiments. He also imported from Spain a new strain of wheat known as Talevera, improved the sub-soil plough and invented a machine for gathering clover heads. Now, you never thought that was important, did you? Joseph Russell's book, A Treatise on the Practice of Chemical Agriculture, published near the end of his life in 1840, was considered revolutionary in its time. "Though this be madness, yet there is method in't."

Cubbington to Offchurch (2.5 miles)

- At end of Church Hill turn left beyond King's Head on to New Street. Where road bends right, go straight ahead on Mill Lane. Where lane bends right, go left on signposted broad track.
- Where track ends, continue ahead on same line, following left field boundary and passing South Cubbington Wood on left and ignoring first plank bridge.
- Continue following left field boundary to reach plank bridge, then go straight ahead over next field.
- On reaching hedge, follow path bending right and descending to footbridge over River Leam.
- Go diagonally right for 30 yards to signpost, then left on wide track to reach farm buildings.
- Just before buildings, at fork in paths, go right through gap in hedge to follow left field boundary to gate into coppice.
- Cross stream and leave coppice through gate to continue ahead, following right field boundary to stile.
- Continue through farmyard of Manor Farm via two stiles then cross field to gate, bringing you into Offchurch with The Stag opposite.
- Go right past The Stag, then first left up School Hill to church.

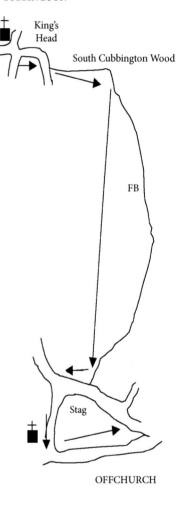

CUBBINGTON

King's Head

South Cubbington Wood

FB

Stag

OFFCHURCH

OFFCHURCH

Offchurch is a tiny village with a fascinating history. It gets its name from the church that the legendary 8th century Mercian king Offa had built here. Offa was king of the Mercians from 757 to 796 AD and was a mighty warrior who united all the Anglo-Saxon tribes of England south of Northumbria by defeating all other leaders in battle. He actually called himself 'rex Anglorum' – the king of the Angles – and, of course, he was responsible for Offa's Dyke, the earthwork believed to stretch from 'sea to sea', South Wales to North Wales.

It is believed that Offa had the church built in order to commemorate his son Fremund who was murdered somewhere between Long Itchington and Harbury and buried at his father's palace in Offchurch. The palace, if it existed, is believed to be on the site of the 17th century Offchurch Bury manor house a short distance to the west of the main village settlement.

A Saxon burial ground was discovered in the nineteenth century to the south of the church, containing weapons and ornaments from about 650 AD. The remains of a stone coffin in St Gregory's church are reputed to be those of Offa's coffin. The church is mainly Norman but has a Saxon feature of a carved serpent above an outside window. "Nothing in his life became him like the leaving it."

THE STAG AT OFFCHURCH

The Stag takes its name from the crest of Sir Edmund Knightley, one of Henry VIII's Commissioners who acquired the estate on the Dissolution of the Monasteries in the 1630s and had a large house built there, now known as Offchurch Bury.

The Stag (01926-425801) has recently, like so many pubs in Warwickshire, been converted into a gastropub but it is open every lunchtime, offering a range of sandwiches and light bites together with Warwickshire Best, Mad Goose and Ubu Real Ales. Get offa your feet for a while.

Offchurch to Harbury (5 miles)

- At T junction at top of hill in Offchurch, beside church of St Gregory, go left on Welsh Road.
- On reaching junction, go right on signposted path descending to bridge over old railway line (National Cycle Network Route 41)
- After bridge, go diagonally right across next field to signpost by large metal gate. Follow path past Fosseway Cottages rising to reach Fosse Way.
- Cross road and go over stile to follow left field boundary over two further stiles and then through two gates beside cottages on to broad track from Bunkers Hill Farm.
- Go left and then right on Welsh Road. Continue on broad road verge to reach crossroads with Ridgeway Lane. Go right, shortly crossing bridge over Grand Union Canal, and eventually emerge at junction with A425.
- Go left into Ufton and take first left on White Hart Lane between White Hart and church of St Michael, passing old stocks, to rejoin A452.
- Go left and just after Village Hall go right on signposted path between houses.
- Continue along right field boundary to gate into edge of Ufton Fields Nature Reserve.
- Go right and follow signposting to road. Go right and, where road bends right, go left through gate straight across field to further gate. Follow left field boundary over several stiles to reach Bull Ring Farm buildings.
- Go left over stile through coppice then right on broad track to cross bridge over railway cutting. Continue on rising surfaced track into Harbury.

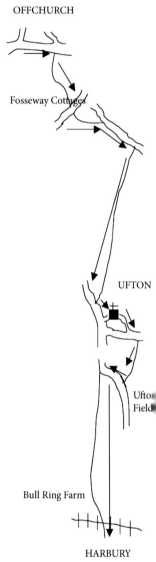

OFFCHURCH

Fosseway Cottages

UFTON

Ufton Field

Bull Ring Farm

HARBURY

UFTON

The village of Ufton, sited unusually on high ground with excellent views over the surrounding countryside and up to the Malvern hills, in Saxon times was under the jurisdiction of Lady Godiva's old man, the Earl of Leofric (what must he have thought of her besporting herself through Coventry?). In the 17th century it was owned by the Spencer family, of Princess Di fame, but the lands were subsequently bequeathed to Balliol College, Oxford, by John Snell, who had purchased it from the Spencers. The Snell Exhibition at Balliol for

Scottish students commemorates this gent; the economist Adam Smith was an early recipient of this award.

By the gateway to St Michael's church is a 14th century preaching cross, which has survived because for many years it lay buried and so preserved. In 1826 it was placed in its present position.

The White Hart (01926-612976) is almost five hundred years old and houses the Ufton Arts Festival, begun in 2009.

"More matter with less art."

UFTON FIELDS

Ufton Fields Nature Reserve is a Site of Special Scientific Interest managed by Warwickshire Wildlife Trust and created from an old limestone quarry. It has a range of pools, bird watching hides and well-maintained and well-signed footpaths to guide you around its environs. The site is noted for its range of

orchids, aquatic species of insects, varied birdlife and butterflies, including rare green and white-letter hairstreaked butterfly species. "One touch of nature makes the whole world kin."

HARBURY PIX

The Gamecock

All Saints

Sail-less Windmill

Old Village Pump

Harbury Plesiausaurus

The Crown

HARBURY STORY

"The name of the village derives from Hereburgh's Byrig, Hereburgh being presumed to be the female leader of an Iron Age tribe who settled at the site around 500 BC."

The village of Harbury has been a settlement on a hill some 400 feet above sea level for 3,000 years. The Romans built the Fosse Way, which forms a boundary of the village, and the remains of a Roman town nearby lie buried beneath the fields. Harbury is mentioned in the Domesday Book and the lands at one time were in the hands of the Knights Templar. The village was known as Hungry Harbury in the 18th and 19th century because it was so poor that people from other neighbouring villages sent food to keep the residents fed in the winter.

The oldest building in Harbury is All Saints church, which was built in the late 13th century but which had to be buttressed in the early 19th century because of its leaning tower. When this didn't work, there was a plan to build a stone steeple to replace the tower but there was not enough money for this so a short brick top was built on the tower. There are several private houses in the village dating back to the 15th and 16th centuries including the first school, the Wagstaffe School, which was founded in 1611. Nearby are the 19th century Wight School, now a chapel, and the sail-less tower of a brick windmill.

Harbury's greatest period of growth was in the 19th century, first of all when quarrying of Blue Lias limestone, used in the making of cement, began and then in the middle of the same century with the construction of the 100 feet Harbury cutting for the GWR Oxford to Birmingham railway line. This latter was at the time the deepest man-made cutting in the world and all dug by hand. These developments help to explain why there are six pubs in the village to quench the sweaty workers' thirst.

Harbury Spoilbank in the spoil left by the digging of the railway cutting to the east of the village is now a SSSI (Site of Special Scientific Interest). It is managed by Warwickshire Wildlife Trust and has become a major butterfly and wildflower habitat.

Harbury expanded significantly in the 20th century with the development of new social housing on its south side and new private housing estates filling in the spaces between the centre of the village and its outskirts. There is now a steady population of 2,500 people. As well as its six pubs, the village has a primary school, a doctor's surgery, a Post Office, two general stores, a chemist, a hairdresser and an estate agent.

HARBURY CELEBRITIES

Harbury Plesiausaurus

In 1928 while digging in a limestone quarry at Harbury, workmen discovered the fossilised remains of a plesiosaurus, a marine reptile from 100 to 200 million years ago. Its skeleton was thin and crumbling – well, it was very old! The bones of the creature stretched twenty-six feet and projecting from the body were four chipped, broken appendages, which paleontologists have termed paddles. The experts noted that the creature had had three eyes, the third in the middle of its small, narrow head, so did they nickname it Isaiah?

Robert Fitz Odo (1160-1247)

Robert Fitz Odo, or Fitz Ooth, was a descendant of Bishop Odo, half-brother of William the Conqueror and the man who commissioned the Bayeux Tapestry. In 1193 there is a record of Robert as lord of Loxley manor near Kenilworth and in 1203 he was living in Harbury, though he had lost his title and become an outlaw. He was given back his lands when Richard the Lionheart returned from his Crusades. It is no surprise then that there are those who claim that Robert Fitz Odo was the original Robin Hood. Go on, sing it – "Robin Hood, Robin Hood, riding through the glen…"

Richard Jago (1715-1781)

The poet Richard Jago was born near Henley-in-Arden and educated at Oxford University where he became friends with the poet William Shenstone and took holy orders. In 1746 he became vicar of Harbury where he served until 1754. He is most remembered for his long poem *Edge Hill, or the rural prospect delineated and moralised*. This long rambling poem in four books describes the famous Civil War battle of 1642. It's easier to visit the site of the battle.

Philip Bushell-Matthews (1943 – present)

Conservative MEP for the West Midlands in 1999 to 2009, Philip Bushell-Matthews became acting leader of the Conservative group at Brussels after Giles Chichester was forced to stand down for misuse of funds. He was previously director of several food manufacturing businesses, including the haute cuisine Red Mill Snacks – manufacturers of Mr. Porky pork scratchings, Transform-a-Snack, Oinks etc. In 2003 he published a light-hearted novel, *The Gravy Train*, about the excesses of the European Parliament. He should know!

HARBURY CAKES

LATESHOP, *High Street*
General provisions, including cakes

THE STORES/POST OFFICE, *Mill Street*
General provisions, including cakes

HARBURY ALE

CROWN INN, *Crown Street*
Olde worlde village pub with beams etc, serving very good, reasonably-priced, home-cooked food and a range of Real Ales. Live music on some evenings.

THE GAMECOCK, *Chapel Street*
Village inn serving fresh, home-cooked food to order. Good selection of Real Ales, including Greene King IPA, Banks's and Old Hooky. Nice garden. Live music and quizzes on certain nights.

THE SHAKESPEARE, *Mill Street*
"The Shake" is a Grade II Listed Building with oak beams and flagstone floors. Newspapers and magazines provided for fireside reading. Restaurant is its speciality but also offers good pub grub. Changing Real Ales served.

THE DOG, *The Bullring*
Brick pub dating from late 19th century. Traditional bar has comfortable furniture and real fire in tiled grate. Serves good, reasonably-priced Indian meals and Real Ales including Greene King IPA, Warden Chaser and Beowulf Noble. Serious dart-playing pub.

THE OLD NEW INN, *Church Street*
Old fashioned country pub with swirly carpet on floors and old pictures on walls. Nothing special but staff are friendly and all village life is there. Nice beer garden at back. Serves range of Church End beers and other Real Ales.

HARBURY ACCOMMODATION

Braeside B&B, 26 Temple End, Harbury, CV33 9NE
(Tel: 01926 613402)

Saddlers Cottage, Chapel Street, Harbury, CV33 9HT
(Tel: 1926 614050)

Model Farm B&B, Bush Heath Road, Harbury, CV33 9JH
(Tel: 01926 613988)

HARBURY SERVICES

Post Office: Mill Street

Banks with ATM: Co-operative outside Lateshop, High Street

Tourist Information Centre: Library, High Street (01926 613297)

Transport connections: regular bus services to Leamington Spa and
Coventry, where there are mainline railway stations.

HARBURY – KINETON

OS Map: Explorer 206

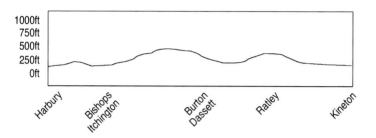

Today's the day when you start to see what Warwickshire calls hills. First it's southwards to Bishop's Itchington, home once to a Petticoat Government, then on through Knightcote to the delights of one of Warwickshire's high points on the Burton Dassett Hills, leading you at their end through Avon Dassett and on to Ratley for a mid-journey break.

Next it's out of Ratley and then through Castle Wood to the folly that is the Castle Inn, with its views over the battlefield of Edgehill that played an indecisive part in the Civil War. The last part of today's trail takes you round the borders of that battlefield and on the extremities of the top-secret munitions dump that is Kineton DSDA and finally into Kineton itself.

PLACE	DAILY MILES	TOTAL MILES
Harbury	-	55
Bishop's Itchington	2	57
Burton Dassett	6.5	61.5
Ratley	10.5	65.5
Kineton	15	70

HARBURY – KINETON
(15 miles)

Harbury – Bishop's Itchington (2 miles)

- From Post Office in Harbury pass Gamecock and continue to end of Chapel Street. Go left and after passing village hall and children's park, go right on signposted path past allotments.
- Go though gate and follow right field boundary to Pineham Farm. Ignore gate to right and go left to gate into farmyard.
- Go left through farmyard on to track. At end of track go left on road. After150 yards go right on signposted path towards Bishop's Itchington.
- Follow right field boundary. Midway through long field go right over two stiles and follow path to footbridge. Continue on rising path to stile (N.B. Bishop's Bowl Lakes away to left).
- Go diagonally right to hedge then take rising path following right field boundary.
- By telegraph poles go right over stile then diagonally right over field to stile and plank bridge over stream.
- Follow right field boundary on rising path through two fields with stiles to emerge on surfaced footpath. Go ahead, via Church Close, into Bishop's Itchington.
- Cross B4451 into Fisher Road and follow road, bending past Butchers Arms. Turn left on Poplar Road and at Post Office go right 50 yards to playing fields.

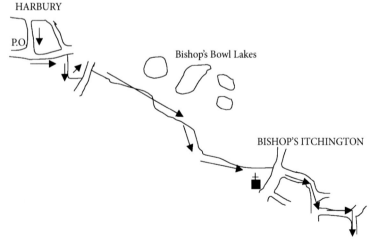

BISHOP'S BOWL LAKES

The five Bishop's Bowl Lakes were created from the old quarries from which Blue Lias limestone was extracted up to 1970 when the company ceased operation. The pools are now used extensively for fishing, both in matches and for pleasure, and are well stocked with carp, tench and barbel. Some of the carp in Blue Pool are over thirty pounds in weight and 'most techniques from legered boilies to floating crust or dog biscuits'

can produce results. Sounds painful. However, there is a café/coffee shop on the site to ease the pain.

The pools are also used for watersports, especially diving, but unfortunately they have become popular with a certain group of youngsters who use them for tombstoning. This dangerous activity, of much concern to local people, involves jumping off a high point into hidden depths with no protection other than wetsuits. It has led to several deaths and serious injuries. "I have a kind of alacrity in sinking."

BISHOP'S ITCHINGTON

This village of two thousand people is situated only two miles from Junction 12 of the M40, which has made it a popular home for commuters working in Birmingham, Leamington or Coventry, although it grew because of the Blue Lias cement works nearby. Its name comes from the River Itchen that flows to the east of the village and its link to the bishops of Lichfield, who were once its landowners. The 19th century St Michael's church was built with Blue Lias limestone. There is one pub, the Butcher's Arms ("If you want to impress your boss, or a consortium of Japanese businessmen, then this is the place for you"), a Post Office and other shops.

In 1949 the village was acclaimed in the press because of its 'Petticoat Government', arising from the situation where six members of the Women's Institute were elected to the Parish Council because of a lack of interest from the men of the village. Happy days.

Bishop's Itchington – Burton Dassett (4.5 miles)

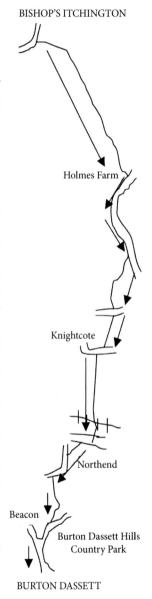

BISHOP'S ITCHINGTON

- Go left through three gates and descend to gate at bottom of field. Go right and follow stream to stile. Continue on path between hedges, to reach footbridge.
- Follow hedge on right to stile then follow left field boundary. At end of field go right 30 yards then left along left field boundary to footbridge. Go straight ahead to stile and continue to gate on left of Holmes Farm to reach road.
- Go right on road. Immediately after hump back bridge go right over stile. Cross field to corner of fence, then go diagonally right to footbridge.
- Go diagonally left to gate and continue to stile in corner of field on to road.
- Cross road to stile and continue over field to next stile. Go diagonally right to stile then through gates by Knightcote House on to road.
- Go right then left opposite Methodist Church into Kimble Close.
- At end of Close go over stile and gate and straight ahead across several fields, usually with stiles between, to reach stile on to railway line.
- Cross railway and stile and go diagonally right to stile and road. Cross road to further stile and go diagonally right again across 2 fields to stile and road in Northend village.
- Go left on rising road into Burton Dassett, passing 1st bus shelter and reach 2nd bus shelter by Old Leys Farm.
- Go left on rising track to gate and continue climbing on path to reach Burton Dassett Beacon and road.

Holmes Farm

Knightcote

Northend

Beacon

Burton Dassett Hills Country Park

BURTON DASSETT

KNIGHTCOTE

This tiny hamlet has a most attractive row of stone-built and thatched cottages in its heart. The Royal Oak pub and the forge are long gone, the latter functioning now as a Post Office, but the Wesleyan Chapel still does business as a Methodist church.

The 17th century manor house is visible across fields to the east. New House Farm to the west houses a collection of seventeen vintage tractors dating back to 1926, most of which are hot bulb tractors, taking 30 minutes to start them using a gas burner. Wow!

BURTON DASSETT HILLS COUNTRY PARK

The hundred-acre Burton Dassett Hills Country Park was created by Warwickshire in 1971 from an area once extensively quarried for ironstone. It is now used much by walkers, picnicker, kite fliers and model glider fliers, these latter attracted by the winds that whip around the hillside. There is an orientation point on Magpie Hill, as well as the tower that is known as The Beacon, though it was probably a windmill in origin. The small wooded site to the south of the site is known as Fox Covert. A Geocache is buried somewhere in the hills.

Although this is not the highest point in the flat county of Warwickshire, it is one of the few hilly parts of the trail. "All that glisters is not gold."

Burton Dassett – Ratley (4 miles)

- Go ahead on road over top of hills, passing car parking payment point. Ignore first road to right and go right at next fork in road, signposted Burton Dassett.
- At further fork go left up to All Saints church. Go through church grounds through two gates and follow path through two further gates. After second gate go left to stile then diagonally left to footbridge.
- Follow left field boundary through three fields with stiles between. Midway through third field go diagonally right to stile. Cross field to gate and lane into Avon Dassett emerging on to road by The Avon.
- Go right on road past The Avon to cross M40. At next crossroads, go straight across and continue on road into Arlescote.
- Go through village, and take second signposted path left towards houses and take left fork through gate into field. Take upper path to climb hill.
- Turn left along fence at top to reach stile on to road. Cross road to gate on right of entrance to shooting range, eventually going right on driveway. Where driveway bears left, go ahead to gate and follow path falling then rising to stile in top corner of field.
- Over stile follow footpath to reach road by Rose & Crown in Ratley.

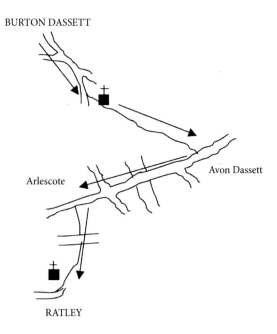

BURTON DASSETT

Avon Dassett

Arlescote

RATLEY

AVON DASSETT

Avon Dassett, the village at the south of the Burton Dassett Hills, was once the home of MP John Profumo, who in 1963 was embroiled in the affair that led to his resignation. The affair involved Profumo himself, at the time Secretary of State for War, the showgirl Christine Keeler and a Russian spy called Yevgeny Ivanov she was also

sleeping with. It forced Profumo to resign and damaged the government's reputation. Prime Minister Harold Macmillan himself resigned some months later, citing ill health, though he lived to a considerable age.

The Avon (01295-690270) is a smashing pub at the heart of the village that is named in the 2010 CAMRA Good Beer Guide. It serves a range of Real Ales, including Timothy Taylor and Greene King, as well as good bar snacks. Its menu is famous for offering "64 ways to eat pie". Go on, try one. "A dish fit for the gods."

RATLEY

Ratley is an old village that sits in a hollow to the east of Edgehill. Most of its houses were built with the Hornton ironstone extracted from the quarries on Edgehill. Its pub, the Rose and Crown (01295-678148), is nine hundred years old and boasts inglenook fireplaces, wooden beams and the ghost of a Roundhead. Darts and Aunt Sally are played here. It serves excellent Real Ales and food and is open daily.

The unusually-named church of St Peter ad Vincula (St Peter in Chains) dates from the 13th century and has a tall preaching cross in its churchyard. Amos John England, the bellringer, was once described by a rector as "an astonishing one-man act on 3 ropes, pulling with both hands and one foot."

Ratley – Kineton (4.5 miles)

- Take road climbing out of Ratley to T junction and go straight across to take signposted footpath descending through woodland on Jacob's Ladder. At bottom of hill take path to left and continue at bottom of woodland to reach fork in paths close to obelisk in field on right. Take left fork climbing to reach Castle Inn (see Battle of Edgehill signage in gardens)

- Take path to right just before Castle Inn and descend to gate and follow right field boundary through gates to join road by Church Farm in Radway. Continue on road through Radway and at fork in roads go left past church. Take second waymarked path on right.

- Go through gates across fields to reach road and straight across through further gate. Go diagonally right to gate in trees then through two fields with gates between to reach road by Westcote Farm.

- Go straight across and follow clearly-marked bridleway across several fields to reach Danger sign for Defence Munitions Depot Kineton. Go left and follow left field boundary round two sides of field to gateway and Ministry of Defence "No Admission without Permission" sign. Go left and follow left field boundary round two sides of field again to gate.

- Continue on path parallel with railway line to gate. Go right across railway line and through gate go left on bridleway. Continue on surfaced track to cross railway line again. At next railway crossing go left on path away from railway line.

- After 200 yards go right on broad bridleway and continue on this track as it winds through fields to emerge by Kineton High School on Banbury Road. Go left into centre of Kineton.

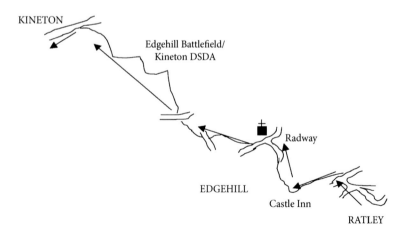

EDGEHILL

The main feature of the village is the Castle Inn (01295-670255), also known as the Round Tower for obvious reasons. It is owned by the Hook Norton brewery and gives splendid views from its garden of the surrounding countryside. The octagonal tower, based on Guy's Tower in Warwick Castle, was designed by local architect Sanderson Millar and was opened in 1750, the anniversary of Oliver Cromwell's death. It is reputed to be the spot where Charles I raised his flag for the first battle of the English Civil War.

At the outbreak of the First World War, Field Marshall Haig, who lived in Radway Grange below here, found his car could not manage the ascent of the hill and was forced to struggle up in reverse gear – a bit like the conduct of the war itself, when you think about it. "Let slip the dogs of war."

BATTLE OF EDGEHILL

Tensions between the intransigent Charles I and his parliament had been rising for some years. By 1642 both sides had amassed large armies and were preparing for a decisive battle. On the 23rd October the Parliamentarians, under the leadership of the Earl of Essex, were gathered at Kineton, while Charles's Royalist troops came together on the ridge of Edgehill. The battle lasted all day and 1500 men were killed in the fighting that ensued but at the end of the day there was no clear winner. Instead the Civil War dragged on for a further four years.

The walk from Edgehill to Kineton is along the route of the modern twenty-mile Battlefields Trail, which includes Edgcote (1469 Wars of the Roses), Cropredy Bridge (1644 Civil War) and Edgehill. Some people claim to hear the voices of the battle still echoing in the fields around. "Uneasy lies the head that wears a crown."

KINETON PIX

St Peter

Cottages in Market Square

Carpenter's Arms

Swan Hotel

War Memorial

Kineton DSDA Hangars

KINETON STORY

"Kineton is in the West Midlands, about as far from the sea as it is possible to get in the 'heart of England'."

Kineton is a large south Warwickshire village situated close to the national watershed. It is the first settlement on the River Dene but its origins are shrouded in mystery. It is believed to have grown as a village in Saxon times and there is a record from 969 of King Edward giving a nobleman called Alfwold land in Cynton. Kineton, or Kington as it was then known, is mentioned in the Domesday Book as having one hundred villagers dwelling therein. On the outskirts of the village are the remains of the earthworks of a motte and bailey castle, known as King John's Castle.

Kineton's next significant moments in history are at the time of the Civil War. The village was looted by Prince Rupert with his Royalist army immediately prior to the indecisive Battle of Edgehill of 1642 that was fought nearby. A year later Charles I met with Queen Henrietta Maria at Kineton to join forces against the Parliamentarians – all to no avail, of course, since he was beheaded shortly afterwards.

During World War 2, Kineton served as a transit camp for Polish and Czechoslovakian troops. At the same time an underground ammunition storage depot was built underneath the fields where the Battle of Edgehill took place. Since then it has been modified and expanded considerably and is now known as Kineton DSDA (Defence Storage and Distribution Agency). The 2,500-acre complex contains twenty-one miles of railway track, hundreds of underground explosives (including nuclear warheads), storehouses and several ammunition processing buildings. It is estimated that it holds something like one-third of a million cubic metres of explosives. It also stores surplus railway trains and carriages. It is one of the most secret places in Britain.

The brownstone St Peter's church in the centre of the village was founded in the 13th century but the nave and chancel were redesigned in the 18th century by noted architect Sanderson Miller. There are several 17th century houses surrounding the secluded Market Square and several Georgian stone houses elsewhere in the village.

Kineton's population nowadays is approximately 2,500. There are some light industries in the village but most local work is in agriculture. Its proximity to Stratford-upon-Avon, Banbury, Leamington Spa and the nearby M40 has made it an attractive commuter village.

KINETON CELEBRITIES

Sir Stephen de Seagrave (? – 1241)

Seagrave was lord of the manor of Kineton and held a market there and a fair on the eve and day of St Peter and St Paul. He became prominent as a justice after the accession of Henry II, acting as one of the regents when Henry was in Brittany in 1230 and being appointed Chief Justiciar in 1232, in which position he acquired considerable wealth. Although he later fell foul of the struggle between Henry and the Lords, losing much of his land, he was eventually restored to position as senior justice.

Sanderson Miller (1716–1780)

Sanderson Miller was an architect who was responsible for the redesign of St Peter's church in Kineton in the 18th century. Miller came from nearby Radway Grange. While studying at Oxford he developed an interest in antiquarianism and a romantic view of the past, which inspired him on inheriting the Radway estate at his father's death to remodel it in the Gothic style. As a result of this he was asked to create the designs for the Shire Hall in Warwick and for Hagley Hall in Worcestershire.

John Newton (1725–1807)

John Newton was the composer of the hymn *Amazing Grace*, written, it is believed, at Christmas 1772 while he was living in Kineton. Newton was initially a slave trader but experienced a religious conversion during a violent storm at sea. On his return to England he married and later became a minister of the church at Olney in Buckinghamshire, despite having no formal qualifications. At Olney he met the poet William Cowper, also a newly-born Christian, and it was from this inspired collaboration that *Amazing Grace* arose.

Daniel Brocklebank (1979 to present)

The actor Daniel Brocklebank was brought up in the area and attended Kineton High School. Always keen on acting through involvement with local drama groups, Daniel's first professional work was as Ralph in the Royal Shakespeare Company's production of *Lord of the Flies* when he was 15. He subsequently appeared in *Shakespeare in Love*, opposite Gwyneth Paltrow and Judi Dench, and *Merlin*. In 2009 he played Brother Jasper and Kaisa in a stage production of Philip Pullman's *His Dark Materials*.

KINETON CAKES

COFFEE STOP & SANDWICH DELI, *Southam Street*
Excellent range of coffees and teas, plus paninis, sandwiches, baguettes, cakes etc..

POST OFFICE, *Banbury Street*
General store as well as Post Office, including choice of cakes.

KINETON ALE

CARPENTERS ARMS, *Banbury Street*
Friendly local pub with open fire and separate public bar. Serves Real Ales including Everards and Little Drinks Co.'s Pilgrim and Buccaneer. No meals served but offers Chinese Take-away within its premises.

SWAN HOTEL, *Banbury Street*
Ancient rambling pub with many rooms, operating since 1682 and serving as local courthouse in 19th century. Offers pool table, darts, juke box and skittle alley upstairs. Bar snacks available plus range of Real Ales.

KINETON ACCOMMODATION

The Old Library, Banbury Street, Kineton, CV35 0JS
(Tel: 01926 640944)

Swan Hotel, Banbury Street, Kineton, CV35 0JS(Tel: 01926 640876)

Smithy Cottage, Radway, Warwick,, CV35 0UN (01295 670095)

The Old Vicarage, Pillerton Hersey, Warwick CV35 0QJ
(01789 740185)

Dockers Barn Farm, Oxhill Bridle Road, Pillerton Hersey, Warwick, CV35 0QB (01926 640475)

KINETON SERVICES

Post Office: Banbury Street

Banks with ATM: HSBC, Kineton Road

Tourist Information Centre: Library, Bridge Street (01926 640285)

Transport connections: regular bus services to Stratford-upon-Avon, Banbury and Leamington Spa, where there are mainline railway stations

KINETON – SHIPSTON-ON-STOUR

OS Maps: Explorer 206 & 205

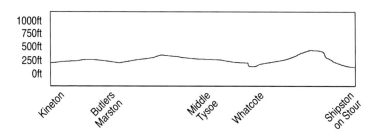

An intriguing exit from Kineton takes you past the mound that was King John's Castle and across country into the old village of Butlers Marston before leading you down the valley of the Red Horse (imagine it filling the hillside!) and eventually into Middle Tysoe, once a huge settlement and sheep market. Then it's across country to see an unusual grave in Oxhill followed by a short trek along a quiet road into Whatcote, where the Royal Oak offers opportunities of a refreshing mid-journey break.

From Whatcote it's a short step to the village of Idlicote then over Idlicote Hill with its lovely views and downhill into the edge of Honington and on into the Cotswold market town of Shipston-on-Stour.

PLACE	DAILY MILES	TOTAL MILES
Kineton	-	70
Butlers Marston	2	72
Middle Tysoe	6.5	76.5
Whatcote	10	80
Shipston-on-Stour	15	85

KINETON to SHIPSTON-ON-STOUR
(15 miles)

Kineton to Butlers Marston (2 miles)

- Leave Kineton on Warwick Road passing St Peter's church and turn left on Castle Road. At end of road go through gate into Dene Valley Park.
- Keep straight ahead on path, passing mound on right that was once King John's Castle then descending through woodland to footbridge.
- Continue on clear path beside sewage works and under railway bridge. After bridge go right over stile then left along left field boundary to gate and footbridge.
- Go straight ahead on rising track across field to stile and shortly after reach surfaced track.
- Go left towards Brookhampton Farm and just before farm entrance go left again on bridleway signposted Mill Farm.
- Continue through grounds of Mill Farm to gate then go diagonally right across field to stile.
- Follow contour of hillside to stile and road. Go right into Butlers Marston.
- Just before War Memorial on right at top of hill, go left on descending stepped path and cross footbridge to reach gate into churchyard.

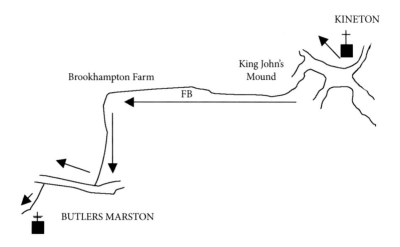

KING JOHN'S MOUND

It is believed that Richard the Lionheart gave the manor of Kineton Magna (variously spelled Kyneton, Kyngton, Chipping Kyneton) to his brother John. When John became king in 1199, he gave the lands to Stephen Seagrave, who had supported him during the Barons Revolt. It is claimed that King John held a Court Leet here during his reign.

Others claim that the castle dates to the reign of King Stephen between 1135 and 1154 – half a century earlier but who knows? And do we really care? Other small castles in the area at Brailes, Halford and Ratley, share similar characteristics as defensive foundations designed to protect the local Anglo-French bigwigs from the Saxon serfs.

The remains of the motte and bailey castle overlook the River Dene to the west of Kineton and are now known as King John's Mound. Until some years ago the area was used as allotments but the Dene Valley Park was created through the enthusiasm of local citizens and its central feature is the curious mound that is King John's Castle. "This castle hath a pleasant seat."

BUTLERS MARSTON

Butlers Marston is only a short distance south west of Kineton on the old salt road from Droitwich to London. It has some attractive grey and brown stone cottages with thatched roofs. The tall-shafted War Memorial is on a small green near the former Gothic school, now a private house. The village used to lie to the east of the church but was evacuated after the Black Death in 1349 and the new village arose where it now stands.

The church of SS Peter & Paul, originally Norman, was drastically restored in 1872 but still retains a Norman arcade and an old octagonal font from the Gothic period. In its churchyard there is an unusual six-sided stone pillar that commemorates members of the Parker family who died between 1928 and 1987.

The mother of William Makepeace Thackeray, the novelist, lived in Butlers Marston before her marriage.

Butlers Marston to Middle Tysoe (4.5 miles)

- Go through churchyard to gate in right corner and descend to footbridge and gate into coppice. Go ahead through coppice then follow left field boundary.
- Where hedge ends, go right on broad track and right again at footpath sign to follow left field boundary to gap in hedge.
- Continue ahead on rising path to fingerpost and then go through gap to follow left field boundary to bottom of field. Go left on track to road by Herd Hill Farm.
- Go right and at summit of Herd Hill go left through gate and diagonally right across field to stile and gate.
- Follow right field boundary to emerge via stiles and gates on A422 by Windmill Farm.
- Go left and just after Springhill Farm go right through gate on signposted path following left field boundary through three fields.
- Mid-way through third field go left through two gates then follow right field boundary through two more fields with gates between.
- At end of next field take left gate over plank bridge then go diagonally right to footbridge in opposite corner.
- Go left alongside sewage works to stile. Then follow left field boundary to double gate.
- Go diagonally right to gate on to broad track and follow into Middle Tysoe, emerging on road by farm buildings.
- Go right on Back Lane to reach Main Street opposite Village Hall.

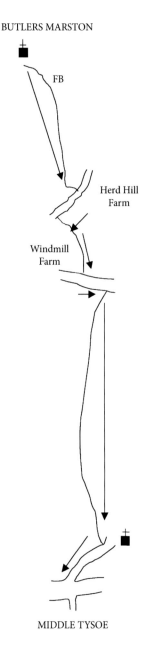

BUTLERS MARSTON

FB

Herd Hill Farm

Windmill Farm

MIDDLE TYSOE

TYSOE

Tysoe is split into three parts – Upper, Middle and Lower. The combined population is about 1200 but in the Middle Ages it was larger than Birmingham with a huge sheep market and many pubs. The only remaining pub is the Peacock Inn in Middle Tysoe. Middle Tysoe also has several shops.

The church of the Assumption of the Blessed Virgin Mary dates back in part to the 11th century, although it has a Saxon wall and there is evidence of pre-Christian Romano-Celtic activity on the site. At the vernal equinox the sun rising over Edge Hill bisects the site of the Red Horse and strikes the centre of the east window.

The church's splendid Norman doorway has a lamb and cross above it, bordered by an older mark and a curious beakhead. "There are more things in heaven and earth, Horatio, than are dreamt of in your philosophy."

RED HORSE OF TYSOE

The Red Horse of Tysoe used to stand proud on the hillside to the east of Lower Tysoe on the Edgehill escarpment. The earliest mention of it is in 1607 but it is likely that it was there long before that, some claiming that it was of Mercian origin. In fact it is quite likely that there have been several Red Horses carved into the red soil of the hillside. It is estimated that the earliest Red Horse may have been one hundred yards long and seventy yards high.

One legend states that it was cut to commemorate the conduct of Richard Nevil, Earl of Warwick, who at the 1461 Battle of Towton had declared his intention of fighting on equal terms with his men and killed his horse with his sword.

The Red Horse of Tysoe

The Red Horse disappeared, however, in 1798 when the land was enclosed and became private. Local residents are currently seeking ways of restoring it.

Middle Tysoe to Whatcote (3.5 miles)

- Go right at crossroads by Village Hall and follow Main Street right through Middle Tysoe as it becomes Upper Tysoe.
- Pass Oxhill Road, Old Tree Lane, and Baldwins Lane and follow road as it bends right to become Shipston Road.
- Continue ahead past Smarts Lane and, where road bends sharply to left, go straight ahead through gates of Tysoe Manor.
- Keep ahead though woodland to gate, then go diagonally right across field to hedge and follow right field boundary.
- Midway through second field go right through gap in hedge then left across next field to footbridge and gate.
- Go straight ahead over field to further gate and continue over next field to fingerpost.
- Go right, following left field boundary and follow bridleway signs to emerge on road at end of driveway to Kirby Farm.
- Go left and follow road into Oxhill to reach church of St Lawrence.
- Continue past church on Green Lane to junction with Whatcote Road. Go left and stay on road to reach Royal Oak in Whatcote.

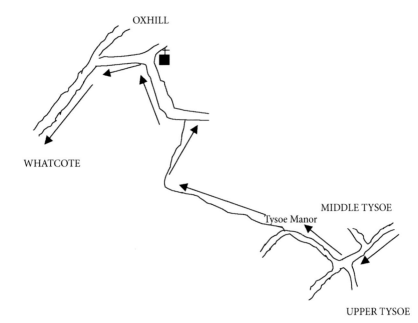

OXHILL

WHATCOTE

MIDDLE TYSOE

Tysoe Manor

UPPER TYSOE

OXHILL

The village of Oxhill, which dates back
to Saxon times, sits midway between
Stratford-upon-Avon and Banbury
in the area known as the Vale of the
Red Horse. It is a thriving village
with a busy local community, its own
newspaper The Oxhill News, the 12th
century church of St Lawrence and
the Peacock pub.

In the churchyard of St Lawrence's church is a most unusual gravestone
to Myrtilla, a "negro slave to Mr Thomas Beauchamp of Nevis", who died
in 1705. Beauchamp was a local man from a family that once owned
Warwick Castle and owned land, probably a sugar plantation, on the
Caribbean island of Nevis. Quite why Beauchamp would have taken so
much trouble to give a proper burial to a black slave girl is impossible to
know, although inevitably there is speculation about the nature of their
relationship.

The Peacock (01295-688060) is a 17th century building that offers good
dining facilities and a range of Real Ales including Timothy Taylor. In 2009
it won the title of Best Newcomer of the Year at the British Pub awards.

WHATCOTE

Whatcote also sits in the Vale of the
Red Horse, its two most prominent
buildings being the 12th century
Norman church of St Peter and the
12th century Royal Oak pub. The
church was massively damaged by a
stray bomb, jettisoned by a German
flier after the great air raid on
Coventry in December 1940. Everything, including the tub font, has been
carefully and faithfully restored

The Royal Oak (01295 680319) claims to be Warwickshire's longest-
established pub, being originally built to house the masons working on
the church. It is built of local stone, covered with ivy and owned by Hook
Norton brewery, so you're sure of a good pint of Real Ale there, and offers
a good range of pub grub. The ideal lunch spot, in fact.

"If music be the food of love, play on."

Whatcote to Shipston-on-Stour (5 miles)

- Continue past Royal Oak through Whatcote and take second road on left. Half way down go right through gate and continue across field to footbridge. Go left through gap in hedge and straight ahead on rising path to marker post.
- Go right 50 yards then left through gap in hedge. Go straight ahead to marker post, then right 50 yards to footbridge. Go right down to road via gate and stile. Go left on road and after 100 yards go right through gate to stile. Go diagonally right on rising path to gate on to road. Go right into Idlicote and left beyond pond.
- Just before church go left on path past house to gate and then further gate to cross road to stile. Continue ahead on rising path to wide track on brow of hill. Go right towards Idlicote Hill Farm.
- Just before farm go left again to end of farm drive and then go right. Follow right field boundary bending right. 100 yards after bend go through gap in hedge and continue descent following left field boundary.
- At end of woodland go sharp left alongside wood. Where hedge comes in from right, go right following right field boundary through two fields. At Hill Clumps woodland go left and follow path winding around edge of woodland. Just before sharp descent, go left across field then right following left field boundary.
- At end of hedge go through gap on left, passing coppice to reach gateway. Go left, following right field boundary descending to bridlepath. Go right on bridlepath and continue descent to reach road at edge of Honington.
- Go left, passing Bowback Manor, and just after crossing bridge over Cod Brook, go through gate on right to pass through grounds of Mill Fell Farm over two footbridges.
- Follow right field boundary through gates to reach A3400. Go left for centre of Shipston-on-Stour.

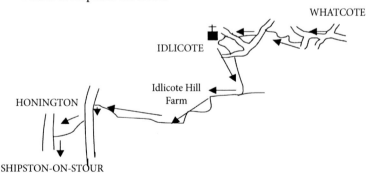

IDLICOTE

Idlicote Hill, one of the spectacular viewing points in this area, was used until 1952 by the Air Ministry as a bombing range. Within the village is the 18th century Idlicote House, once moated, used during the Second World War by the Women's Land Army and subsequently as a boys' school, though it is now privately owned. The Norman church of St James the Great has an unusual three-decker pulpit, a 12th century Norman doorway and memorials to a local family with connections to the East India Company.

Elspeth Howe, wife the former Chancellor of the Exchequer Geoffrey Howe, was chair of the Equal Opportunities Commission in the late 1970s and later Chair of the Broadcasting Standards Commission. She was made Baroness Howe of Idlicote in 2001. As a result of Geoffrey having been knighted and later made a peer and her own ennoblement, she is once, twice, three times a lady – Lady Howe, Lady Howe of Aberavon and The Lady Howe of Idlicote.

HONINGTON

Yet another old unspoiled village recorded in the Domesday Book, Honington is thought to owe its name to the production of honey hereabouts. Its principal building Honington Hall was built by a wealthy London merchant Sir Henry Parker in 1682. It is known for some of its (and his) extravagances – busts of Roman emperors set above the ground-floor windows and an octagonal saloon with a ceiling attributed to Bellucci.

Not content with these, the noble knight created a monument of himself and his son dressed in costumes and wigs and conversing animatedly inside All Saints church. This oddity fits well with the tablet to Joseph Townsend that features a naked boy, described as "perhaps the most unpleasant cherub in England". In the churchyard is the gravestone of Mary Townsend, who founded the Girls' Friendly Society in 1875. "A long farewell to all my greatness!"

SHIPSTON-ON-STOUR PIX

Black Horse

Mrs Brown's Teahouse

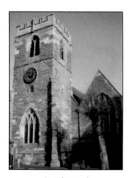

St Edmund

The George Hotel

Edward Sheldon Wine Merchant

Shipston Bridge

SHIPSTON-ON-STOUR STORY

"A hidden treasure nestled in a picturesque valley on the edge of the Cotswolds."

Shipston-on-Stour is a small town of mainly Georgian buildings, though its origins lie probably before the arrival of the Romans. It was sufficiently well established by the 8th century for it to become a gift to the Bishop of Worcester from the Saxon Uhtred. It became known as Sheep Wash Town because the River Stour was used for washing sheep in early summer, and is recorded in the Domesday Book as Scepwaeisctune. Mop Fairs, still held in June and October, originated in the 13th century when a charter was obtained by the local Prior and the first bridge was built in 1280, when the modern pattern of the town became established.

The development of the Cotswold wool trade in medieval times led to Shipston-on-Stour's prosperity, with two of its main economic activities being spinning and weaving. By the end of the 17th century a large organisation employing home workers in the manufacture of woollen velvet (known as "shag") had been built up by a certain John Hart, whose memorial is in St Edmund's church.

Shipston-on-Stour's geographical position made it an important coaching stop for merchants, which goes some way to explaining the large number of inns in the town. The coming of the railways had a major impact on the town's prosperity, however, and its current status as a thriving small market town on the edge of the Cotswolds owes much to the range of independent traders that have taken root there and the attractiveness of its buildings in its three main thoroughfares – High Street, Church Street and particularly Sheep Street.

St Edmund's church has a 15th century brownstone tower but the rest of the building is from 1855, designed by G.E. Street – a design that Pevsner is sniffy about ("considering what he was capable of, very disappointing"). Its graveyard displays the arms of Jesus College, Oxford, patrons of the church when the town became an independent parish in 1719.

The Bee Gees' Robin Gibb sang of "Cold be my days in Shipston-on-Stour" in his 1970 solo album *Sing Slowly Sisters.* In a radio interview in May 2007 he explained that this related to his youthful experiences, riding horses with his brother Barry. Sadly the album was never released, so we'll probably never know the truth of this!

SHIPSTON-ON-STOUR CELEBRITIES

Richard Hyckes (1524-1621)
The magnificent and rare Sheldon Tapestries, skilfully hand-woven out of wool, emanated from the work of Richard Wyckes who lived in the hamlet of Barcheston just outside Shipston-on-Stour. Wyckes was sent by his master William Sheldon to the Low Countries to study the craft of weaving and returned with a coterie of Flemish weavers. Between them they created these wonderful works of art, highly stylised tapestries with floral decorations and mythological motifs. They were initially hung in Sheldon's home, Weston Manor, and became very fashionable in their time. Hyckes was commissioned to make tapestries for the Earl of Leicester and for Elizabeth I.

Edward Sheldon (1800s)
Edward Sheldon took over as vintner in the 1850s from his uncle Richard Badger. Under Sheldon the business grew and grew, supplying wines throughout the country and to many parts of the British Empire. Vintage port, sherry and madeira were shipped to Warwickshire's wealthy country houses, to officers' messes in the United Kingdom and abroad, and to universities. Edward Sheldon Independent Wine Merchants still operates from the same premises.

Francis Haverfield (1860-1919)
Francis Haverfield, one of the great authorities on Roman Britain, was born in the town, son of the local minister. Haverfield redefined the study of Roman archaeology, as it was then understood in Britain. He was appointed Camden Professor of Ancient History at Oxford University in 1907 and systematically set about changing prevailing views of Roman Britain through thorough research and professionally-organised excavations. His scholarship is still valued today.

Cy Endfield (1914-1995)
Cy Endfield attended Yale University, where he developed an abiding interest in magic and card tricks. It was this skill that attracted him as a young actor to Orson Welles who employed him in his film production company. In 1951 Endfield was identified as a Communist by HUAC and, rather than submit to blacklisting, he came to Britain where he stayed for the rest of his life. He made a number of films under false names to avoid distribution problems but his finest film was *Zulu*, the film that gave Michael Caine his big break. He died of cardio-vascular disease in Shipston-on-Stour.

SHIPSTON-ON-STOUR CAKES

MRS BROWN'S TEAROOM, *High Street*
Award-winning traditional tearoom with comfortable ambience. Offers sandwiches, salads, homemade cakes, cream teas, speciality teas, and Fairtrade coffees.

THE BAKERY, *Sheep Street*
As the name suggests, situated in the bakery so always smelling of fresh bread. Offers sandwiches, baguettes, baps, paninis, teas and coffees.

SHIPSTON-ON-STOUR ALE

THE FALCON HOTEL, *Church Street*
Re-opened in 2002 as café bar and at the time locally known as 'Pink Parrot' because of colour of exterior walls. Serves lunches and evening meals and Real Ales including Adnams, Hook Norton and Ansells, plus Weston's Old Rosie cider.

WHITE BEAR, *High Street*
Cheerful pub with newspapers on sticks and cricket memorabilia. Serves lunches and evening meals (not Sun). Real Ales include Adnams and Hook Norton.

BLACK HORSE, *Station Road*
Ancient stone-built pub with thatched roof, dating back to 1540. Cosy and welcoming lounge. Pub games, including Aunt Sally, crib and dominoes, played. Homemade food available (not Sun eve). Serves Everards, Greene King IPA and Abbot Real Ales. In CAMRA national guide.

HORSESHOE INN, *Church Street*
Old black and white coaching inn recently re-opened after flooding damage. U-shaped bar and inglenook fireplace. Food available (not Sun eve). Serves Ruddles and changing local Real Ales.

SHIPSTON-ON-STOUR ACCOMMODATION

Shipston Guest House, 42 Church Street, Shipston-on-Stour, CV36 4AS (Tel: 01608 661002)

Holly End, London Road, Shipston-on-Stour, CV36 4EP (Tel: 01608 664064)

Harrow Hill House, Malthouse Lane, Shipston-on-Stour, CV36 5JL (Tel: 01608 684004)

George Hotel, High Street, Shipston-on-Stour, CV36 4AJ (Tel: 01608 661453)

White Bear, High Street, Shipston-on-Stour, CV36 4AJ (Tel: 001608 661558)

Falcon Hotel, Church Street, Shipston-on-Stour, CV36 (Tel: 01608 664414)

SHIPSTON-ON-STOUR SERVICES

Post Office: High Street

Banks with ATM: Lloyds and HSBC in town centre.

Tourist Information Centre: Library, Church Street (Tel: 01608 661255)

Transport connections: regular bus service to Banbury and Stratford-upon-Avon, where there are mainline railway stations.

SHIPSTON-ON-STOUR – STRATFORD-UPON-AVON

OS Map: Explorer 205

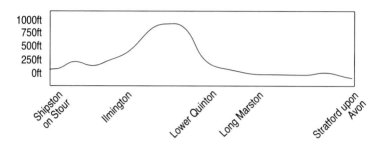

The final section of the trail takes you north-west out of Shipston-on-Stour to another hilly point near the charming village of Ilmington, famous for its Morris Dancers and the intrigues within its church. A further cross-country walk on the Centenary Way brings you along the side of Meon Hill, a superstitious place in times gone by, and into Lower Quinton, where the College Arms recalls the village's old-time ownership. From Lower Quinton it's a short hop across fields to the south of an ex-airfield now used for Drag-racing and much else to the edge of Long Marston, where the Mason's Arms offers a final opportunity for refreshment before reaching the end of your journey.

The Greenway, formerly the Honeybourne railway, provides a steady and easy last part of your journey, returning you to Stratford-upon-Avon, hopefully a wiser and fitter person.

PLACE	DAILY MILES	TOTAL MILES
Shipston-on-Stour	-	85
Ilmington	4.5	89.5
Lower Quinton	7.5	92.5
Long Marston	9.5	94.5
Stratford-upon-Avon	15	100

SHIPSTON-ON-STOUR to STRATFORD-UPON-AVON (15 miles)

Shipston-on-Stour to Ilmington (4.5 miles)

- Leave Shipston-on-Stour via A3400 going north and follow for approximately a mile and a half. Just after Puckpits Farm go through gate on left and go diagonally right across field to gate.
- Follow left field boundary on rising track through two fields with gate between. At end of second field go through gap in hedge and follow right field boundary descending to gate on to A429 (Fosse Way).
- Go straight across on to road signposted Blackwell. Continue on road through Blackwell village, going over two sets of crossroads then left at T junction. 400 yards beyond the village go right on road and after 100 yards go left over stile and follow left field boundary to stile.
- Go diagonally right across next field to stile in opposite corner by willow trees. Go diagonally right again across next field to hedge and follow right field boundary to stile.
- Continue on same line following right field boundary to stile on to road at junction. Go straight across on to road signposted Ilmington. After 100 yards take signposted path to right rising over hill (aim between telegraph poles) to stile.
- Continue across field to stile into Ilmington. Go straight across on to Middle Street, passing Howard Arms and village shop and continue as road becomes footpath, bending right by pond and going round left side of church to reach road.

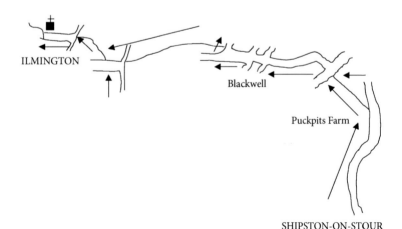

ILMINGTON

Blackwell

Puckpits Farm

SHIPSTON-ON-STOUR

ILMINGTON

Ilmington is a large Cotswold village of honey-coloured stone houses standing on the Ilmington Downs hills, whereon is Warwickshire's highest point at 850 feet. Just to the west of the village is Newfoundland Well, where a well discovered in 1684 gave false hopes of developing Ilmington as a spa town. There are two pubs in the village, the Red Lion and the Howard Arms.

The church of St Mary the Virgin contains 1930s pews carved by Yorkshire master-craftsman Robert Thompson, a.k.a. The Mouseman because his signature was a carved mouse (there are eleven mice in the church). In the churchyard are twelve lime trees, representing the apostles, and the

grave of Dorothy Hodgkin, who was awarded the Nobel prize for Chemistry in 1964 and lived in the village.

One of the treasures inside the church is the Apple Map, inspired by the artist and gardener June Hudson.

ILMINGTON MORRIS MEN

The Ilmington Morris Men began dancing in the 17th century and they're still at it. The Arthurs family had a long tradition with the Morris men, Tom Arthurs still dancing at the age of eighty-five. He taught the Ilmington tunes to a certain Sam Bennett, who was central to the group in the early part of the

twentieth century and who was recorded by the folk song collector Cecil Sharp. His headstone in the churchyard has a violin carved on it. It was Sam Bennett who introduced the Hobby Horse to the Ilmington Morris men and it still survives, much patched up but believed to be the oldest in the country.

There are twenty-four Ilmington dances, including the linked handkerchief dance Maid of the Mill, the stick dance The Jubilee and the unusual Broom Dance. The latter is danced by one man with a household broom to the tune of Greensleeves. The Ilmington Morris men meet in the Red Lion. "In the prime of his dancing days."

Ilmington to Lower Quinton (3 miles)

- Go left on road (Back Street) and at junction with Campden Hill go right. After 200 yards go right on stepped path to stile. Follow right field boundary through two fields with stiles.
- At second stile go diagonally left to gap in hedge. Go left then diagonally right, following yellow poles descending and rising to stile (N.B. views of Warwickshire).
- Go left and follow left field boundary to gate. Continue ahead on clear path descending to gate with pool on right. Follow left field boundary rising to gate on right into driveway. Follow driveway to road and go right.
- At T junction go left and left again at next junction. Just after Adlington Lane Units go right over stile and follow right field boundary.
- Where hedge ends, go diagonally left to post then follow left field boundary round two sides of field to footbridge. Follow right field boundary to gate then go diagonally right on rising path through field to stile on to road.
- Go right and immediately left on driveway to Meon Hall. Just before Hall gates go right through gate and follow signposts descending and rising to gate.
- Go straight ahead over field to double stile. Go right to double stile then follow left field boundary to gate. Go diagonally right descending to stile in opposite corner leading to gate.
- Go diagonally left to find stile and path between houses to road. Go right into Upper Quinton. After The Green go right to reach crossroads in Lower Quinton.

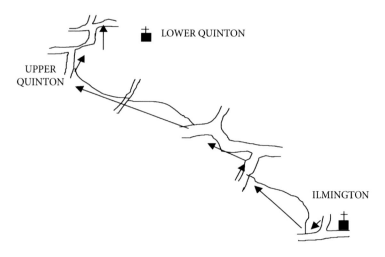

LOWER QUINTON

UPPER QUINTON

ILMINGTON

LOWER QUINTON

Lower Quinton, at the foot of the Cotswold hills is an old village found in the Domesday Book that later became the property of Magdalen College in Oxford. Hence the stonebuilt, double-gabled College Arms (01789-720342) which serves a range of Real Ales, including Hook Norton and Wye Valley, plus good pub grub. Its pub sign is the college's coat of arms.

The 12th century Norman church of St Swithun has a huge 127 feet spire, visible for miles around. Inside is a 12th century circular font and amidst the pews an effigy of Sir William Clopton who fought at the Battle of Agincourt ("Once more unto the breach, dear friends...") and whose wife Joanna's table-tomb is in the St Anne's chapel within the church, proclaiming that she had become a nun after his death in order to devote herself to good works. Altogether now, aaah!!!!

WITCHCRAFT AND MEON HILL

Just opposite St Swithun's is a cottage where farm labourer Charles Walton lived. Walton was a reclusive character but was known for his way with animals and for being a clairvoyant. Some villagers thought that he meddled in witchcraft and Meon Hill to the south of the village has been the subject of devilish deeds and hauntings for centuries.

On St Valentine's Day 1945 Charles Walton set out to work on Meon Hill but never returned. He was found pinned to the ground with his own pitchfork, his throat cut with his own sickle and the sign of the cross carved into his chest.

Inspector Fabian of Scotland Yard (yes, the original "Fabian of the Yard" later immortalised on TV driving at speed in his Humber Hawk to solve gruesome crimes) was summoned but failed to solve the mystery. To this day no-one has ever been charged with Charles Walton's murder. "Double, double toil and trouble."

Lower Quinton to Long Marston (2 miles)

- Continue over crossroads on to Aylstone Close. Just before road bends to right, take footbridge on left and follow path between fence and hedge to gate.
- Cross field to gate and stile and continue on same line to footbridge and stile.
- Go left following left field boundary and stream through three fields with gates between to reach gate on to B4632.
- Go straight across to stile and continue across field to gate. 20 yards after gate take stile on right then go left, following left field boundary to stile.
- Go right on clear path between fence and hedge around two sides of field and continuing up to stile (N.B. Shakespeare County Raceway to right).
- Go straight ahead on broad track passing pool on right and follow to reach Greenway (old railway line).
- Go across Greenway on to surfaced track leading to Long Marston.
- Take second right road to find shops and Mason's Arms for a final pint before reaching the end of your journey.

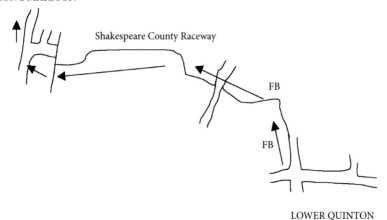

LONG MARSTON

Shakespeare County Raceway

FB

FB

LOWER QUINTON

LONG MARSTON

The village of Long Marston is the "dancing Marston" of the rhyme attributed to Shakespeare (remember that?). It has a village shop, the Poppin Stores, run by a co-operative of village people and housing the Post Office, the excellent Mason's Arms (01789-720586) which is owned by Hook Norton Brewery and has a skittle alley, and the church of St James the Great built in the 14th century.

After his defeat at Battle of Worcester. King Charles fled south disguised as a servant, Will Jackson, to Mistress Jane Lane. They stayed at the Manor House, now known as King's Lodge, and Charles was ordered to wind the meat-jack and was beaten by the cook for his incompetence at this simple task.

Just to the east of the village is Long Marston Airfield which was an RAF Bomber Command training until it closed in 1954. It is now the site of the Shakespeare County Raceway for dragracing, the second largest such strip in the United Kingdom. It also hosts the Bulldog Bash Bikers Festival. "This is a sorry sight."

MIDDLE QUINTON ECO- TOWN

In 2008 the UK government announced its intention of creating a number of eco-towns and one of the sites chosen was the former Royal Engineers depot at Middle Quinton between Lower Quinton and Long Marston. The proposal was for a town with 6,000 zero carbon homes, including 2,000 affordable houses, and an infrastructure that included up to four schools, health care and retail facilities.

The plan was not popular with local residents, who mounted a campaign called BARD (Better Accessible Responsible Development), and got the support of Dame Judi Dench and John Nettles. County and District Councils also opposed it. In 2009 four sites in England were named for the development of eco-towns; Middle Quinton was not one of them but it is still apparently under consideration. "Out, damned spot!"

Long Marston to Stratford-upon-Avon (5.5 miles)

- Retrace steps from Long Marston, going left on Wyre Lane to reach Greenway.
- Go left and follow Greenway towards Stratford-upon-Avon.
- Cross road at Milcote by Carriages Café.
- Just before railway bridge go sharp right down to gate. Go left to further gate.
- Continue on right bank of River Avon, going under road bridge and passing weirs, into recreation ground opposite Royal Shakespeare Theatre.
- Follow path up to bridge and go left into centre of Stratford-upon-Avon.

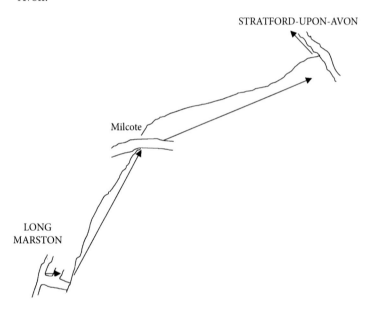

STRATFORD-UPON-AVON PIX

William Shakespeare

Shakespeare's Birthplace

"O noble fool! O worthy fool!"

Harvard House

Guildhall

Shakespeare's Tomb

STRATFORD-UPON-AVON STORY

"To appreciate Stratford-upon-Avon one has to make the gigantic effort of forgetting Shakespeare and the pilgrims and the trippers..."

Nikolaus Pevsner

You would be hard pressed to think of Stratford-upon-Avon without thinking of Shakespeare but let's give it a try. The town was originally a Saxon settlement that grew in importance in the 12th century when it was granted the right to hold its own market. By the 13th century it had its own grammar school, later attended by you know who, and remained an important market town, specialising in the trading of sheep's wool and leather tanning, until the late 18th century. It was in 1769 that its fortunes began to change, when the very first Shakespeare Jubilee Festival was held, largely through the efforts of actor David Garrick. From then on, Stratford began to become a tourist hub. Nowadays it receives upwards of three and a half million visitors a year.

It is difficult to wander around Stratford without being reminded of the Brad (sorry, Bard!), from the rebuilding of the Royal Shakespeare Theatre on the banks of the Avon to the houses with genuine Shakespeare associations. That's not to mention the many businesses that have hijacked his name or his reputation or his characters, such as Falstaff's Antiques, Iago Jewellers or Much Ado about Toys, nor the many statuary or written tributes around the town, such as the metallic jester on Henley Street.

However, there are other interesting sites in Stratford. On High Street is the delightful black and white Elizabethan Harvard House with the date 1596 on it. This was the home of John Harvard, whose wealth founded Harvard University in the USA. The 15th century Guildhall in Church Street is now part of the grammar school.

But back to Our Bill. The first permanent theatre in Stratford was the Shakespeare Memorial Theatre of 1879, sponsored by local brewer Charles Flower. This theatre burned down in 1926 and productions had to continue in a local cinema. In 1932 the new Shakespeare Memorial Theatre opened and over the next thirty years established an enviable reputation for the quality of its work, attracting the likes of John Gielgud, Laurence Olivier, Peggy Ashcroft and Ralph Richardson to perform there. In 1960 Peter Hall formed the Royal Shakespeare Company and a year later the theatre was renamed the Royal Shakespeare Theatre. In 2007 the rebuilding of the theatre commenced, with productions taking place in the temporary Courtyard Theatre.

STRATFORD-UPON-AVON CELEBRITIES

William Shakespeare (1564-1616)
Yes, the original Swan of Avon, a.k.a. the Bard, came from here, as if you didn't know. The house where he was born is in Henley Street and home to the Shakespeare Birthplace Trust. Will attended Stratford Grammar School, married Anne Hathaway, seven years older than himself, when he was eighteen but, of course, he won his fame in London, primarily as an actor and then as an actor-manager and playwright. His thirty-seven plays range from farce through light romance to high tragedy and contain language which has penetrated so much of our own daily discourse. No fool, he made a fortune and retired to Stratford where he died.

David Garrick (1717-1779)
Although David Garrick came originally from Lichfield and made his name at the Theatre Royal, Drury Lane in London, he is widely credited with making Stratford synonymous with Shakespeare-worship. The most gifted actor of his time, Garrick was renowned for his Shakespearean roles, and in 1769 he launched the very first Shakespeare Jubilee Festival. The town has never been the same since, even though much of the original festival was washed out by heavy rain. On that day bardolatry was born!

Marie Corelli (1855-1924)
Marie Corelli was born Mary Mackay, the illegitimate daughter of a Scottish poet. Her professional life was originally as a pianist, but she turned to writing romantic fiction, publishing her first novel, *A Romance of Two Worlds*, in 1886. Thereafter she churned out melodramatic novels at the rate of roughly one a year. In 1901, by now a highly-successful bestseller, she moved to Stratford, where she had her own gondola, complete with gondolier, on the River Avon.

Arthur C. Clarke (1917-2008)
Arthur C. Clarke, the science fiction writer most famous for writing the novel *2001: A Space Odyssey*, served in the Royal Air Force in the early development of radar at Stratford during the Second World War. After the war he became chairman of the British Interplanetary Society and proposed the use of geostationary satellite systems as telecommunication systems; at the same time he began to publish science fiction stories in popular magazines. From 1956 to his death Clarke lived in Sri Lanka.

STRATFORD-UPON-AVON CAKES

AS YOU LIKE IT, *Henley Street*
Small but intimate café, offering homemade cakes, plus range of teas and coffees. Can get busy.

COURTYARD THEATRE CAFE, *Southern Lane*
At the heart of the theatre complex the RSC café serves sandwiches, light meals, cakes, using local ingredients, plus a good range of teas and coffees.

HATHAWAY TEAROOMS, *High Street*
Characterful café overlooking High Street up creaky stairs from bakery. Serves fresh homemade scones and cakes plus cream teas and range of teas and coffees.

STRATFORD-UPON-AVON ALE

GARRICK, *High Street*
Building dates from 1594 but used as pub since 1718. Named after actor David Garrick who initiated the annual Shakespeare Birthday Celebrations in 1769. Always busy. Sandwiches and meals available all day. Real Ales include Greene King and Morland.

QUEENS HEAD, *Ely Street*
18th century pub with exposed beams, stone-flagged floor, fires and L-shaped bar. Evening meals at weekends only. Real Ales include Adnams, Bass, Shepherd Neame and Charles Wells, plus Thatchers cider.

WINDMILL, *Church Street*
In business since 1599 and claims to be Stratford's oldest pub. Timber-framed building with low ceilings and big log fire. Evening meals available plus Real Ales including Flowers, Greene King and Ruddles.

PEN & PARCHMENT, *Bridgefoot*
Well restored after 2007 floods with bare floorboards or flagstones. Offers Greene King, Abbot and Timothy Taylor. Good value food available all day. Views of canal basin.

STRATFORD-UPON-AVON ACCOMMODATION

Adelphi Guest House, 39 Grove Road, Stratford, CV37 6PB
(Tel: 01789 204469)

Ambleside Guest House, 41 Grove Road, Stratford, CV37 6PB
(Tel: 01789 297239)

Applegarth, Warwick Road, Stratford, CV37 6YW
(Tel: 01789 267488)

Curtain Call Guest House, 142 Alcester Road, Stratford, CV37 9DR
(Tel: 01789 267734)

Emsley Guest House, 4 Arden Street, Stratford-, CV37 6PA
(Tel: 01789 299557)

Forget Me Not House, 18 Evesham Place, Stratford, CV37 6HT
(Tel: 01789 204907)

Hunters Moon Guest House, 150 Alcester Road, Stratford, CV37 9DR
(Tel: 01789 292888)

Linhill Guest House, 35 Evesham Place, Stratford, CV37 6HT
(Tel: 01789 292879)

Salamander Guest House, 40 Grove Road, Stratford, CV37 6PB
(Tel: 01789 205728)

Stretton House, 38 Grove Road, Stratford, CV37 6PB
(Tel: 01789 268647)

Virginia Lodge, 12 Evesham Place, Stratford, CV37 6HT
(Tel: 01789 292157)

STRATFORD-UPON-AVON SERVICES

Post Office: Henley Street

Banks with ATM: Barclays, HSBC, Lloyds and NatWest in town centre.

Tourist Information Centre: 62 Henley Street (Tel: 01789 264293)

Transport connections: mainline railway station.

USEFUL INFORMATION

Tourist Information Centres

Stratford-upon-Avon, Henlet Street (Tel: 01789 264293)

Alcester, Library, Priory Road, (Tel: 01789 762430)

Henley-in-Arden, Library in Guildhall, High Street (01564 792965)

Kenilworth, Library, Smalley Place (01926 748900)

Harbury, Library, High Street (01926 613297)

Kineton, Library, Bridge Street (01926 640285)

Shipston-on-Stour, Library, Church Street (01608 661255)

Other Contacts

National Rail Enquiries (Tel: 08457 484950)

West Midlands Traveline (Tel: 0871 200 2233)

www.shakespeare-country.co.uk

www.enjoywarwickshire.com

www.stratford-upon-avon.co.uk

www.alcester.co.uk

www.henley-in-arden.org

www.kenilworthweb.co.uk

www.shipstononline.org

SUGGESTED READING

Allen, Geoff (2000), *Warwickshire Towns and Villages*, Sigma

Anon (1999), *Kineton, the Village and its History*, Kineton & District Local History Group

Bullen, Annie & Royston, Angela (2004), *Stratford-upon-Avon: More than a Guide*, Pitkin Publishing

Cooper, William (1946), *Henley-in-Arden: An Ancient Market Town and its Surroundings*, Cornish Books

Deary, Terry (2006), *Stratford-upon-Avon* (Horrible Histories), Scholastic

Griffin, Vivienne M. (1986), *Shipston-on-Stour from old photographs*, Warwickshire County Library

Hunter, Robert E. (2009), *Shakespeare and Stratford-upon-Avon*, C.U.P.

James, Peter (1980), *Icetone: The Story of a Warwickshire Village*, Unknown

Mee, Arthur (1936), *The King's England: Warwickshire*, Hodder & Stoughton

Palmer, Roy (1994), *The Folklore of Warwickshire*, Llanerch Press

Pevsner, Nikolaus & Wedgwood, Alexandra (1966), *The Buildings of England: Warwickshire*, Penguin

Saville, G. Edward (1986), *Alcester: A History*, Brewin

Scott, Christopher L., Turton, Alan & Arni, Eric Gruber von Dr. (2006) *Edgehill: The Battle Reinterpreted*, Leo Cooper Ltd

Scott, Sir Walter (2006), *Kenilworth: A Romance*, Penguin

Tyack, Geoffrey (1994), *Warwickshire Country Houses*, Phillimore & Co

Warwickshire Federation of Women's Institutes (2000), *The Warwickshire Village Book*, Countryside Books

DISTANCE CHECKLIST

SECTION ONE	DAILY MILES	TOTAL MILES
STRATFORD-UPON-AVON	-	-
Welford-on-Avon	4.5	4.5
Bidford-on-Avon	8	8
Wixford	11.5	11.5
ALCESTER	14	14

SECTION TWO	DAILY MILES	TOTAL MILES
ALCESTER	-	14
Coughton	3.5	17.5
Studley	6	20
Ullenhall	9.5	23.5
HENLEY-IN-ARDEN	14	28

SECTION THREE	DAILY MILES	TOTAL MILES
HENLEY-IN-ARDEN	-	28
Lowsonford	3	31
Baddesley Clinton	6	34
Five Ways	8.5	36.5
KENILWORTH	13.5	41.5

SECTION FOUR	DAILY MILES	TOTAL MILES
KENILWORTH	-	41.5
Stoneleigh	3	44.5
Cubbington	6	47.5
Offchurch	8.5	50
HARBURY	13.5	55

SECTION FIVE	DAILY MILES	TOTAL MILES
HARBURY	-	55
Bishop's Itchington	2	57
Burton Dassett	6.5	61.5
Ratley	10.5	65.5
KINETON	15	70

SECTION SIX	DAILY MILES	TOTAL MILES
KINETON	-	70
Butlers Marston	2	72
Middle Tysoe	6.5	76.5
Whatcote	10	80
SHIPSTON-ON-STOUR	15	85

SECTION SEVEN	DAILY MILES	TOTAL MILES
SHIPSTON-ON-STOUR	-	85
Ilmington	4.5	89.5
Lower Quinton	7.5	92.5
Long Marston	9.5	94.5
STRATFORD-UPON-AVON	15	100